Cute & Easy Cake Toppers! Shoes, Bags, Make-up and more!
Mini Fashions That Look Good Enough To Eat!

Contributors

Following a career in finance, Amanda Mumbray launched her cake business in 2010 and has gone from strength to strength, delighting customers with her unique bespoke creations and winning several Gold medals at various International Cake Shows. Amanda's **Clever Little Cupcake** company is based near Manchester, UK: **www.cleverlittlecupcake.co.uk**

Lesley Grainger has been imaginative since birth and has baked since she was old enough to hold a spatula. When life-saving surgery prompted a radical rethink, Lesley left a successful corporate career to pursue her passion for cake making. Lesley is based in Greenock, Scotland. Say 'hello' at: **www.lesleybakescakes.co.uk**

First published in 2014 by Kyle Craig Publishing

Editor: Alison McNicol

Design and illustration: Julie Anson

ISBN: 978-1-908-707-45-1

A CIP record for this book is available from the British Library.

A Kyle Craig Publication

www.kyle-craig.com

Contents

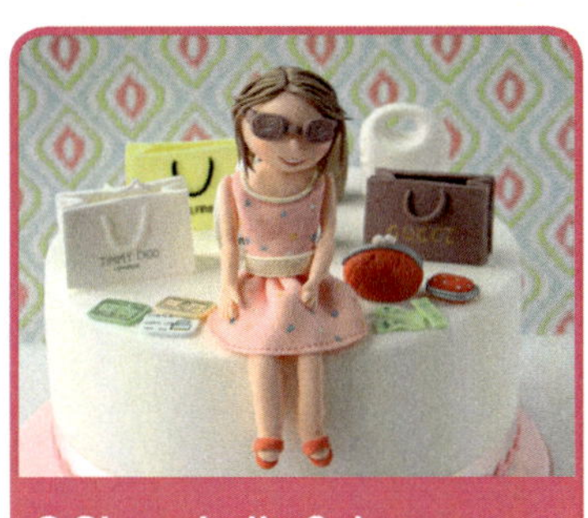

Welcome!

Welcome to **'Passion for Fashion'**, the latest title in the **Cute & Easy Cake Toppers** Collection.

Each book in the series focuses on a specific theme, and here we have compiled a fun and fashionable selection of mini shoes, handbags, shopping bags, make-up, gadgets and fashion-friendly toppers, perfect for any adorable divas or fabulous fashionistas!

Whether you're an absolute beginner or an accomplished cake decorator, these projects are suitable for all skill levels, and we're sure that you will have as much fun making them as we did!

Enjoy!

Fondant/Sugarpaste/Gumpaste

Fondant/Sugarpaste – Ready-made fondant, also called ready to roll icing, is widely available in a selection of fantastic colours. Most regular cake decorators find it cheaper to buy a larger quantity in white and mix their own colours using colouring pastes or gels. Fondant is used to cover entire cakes, and as a base to make modelling paste for modelling and figures (see below).

Modelling Paste – Used throughout this book. Firm but pliable and dries faster and harder than fondant/sugarpaste. When making models, fondant can be too soft so we add CMC/Tylose powder to thicken it.

Florist Paste/Gumpaste –The large and small shoes in this book are made using florist paste as it is more pliable than fondant, but dries very quickly and becomes quite hard, so it is widely used for items like flowers that are delicate but need to hold their shape when dry.

Florist Paste can be bought ready made, or you can make at home by adding Gum-Tex/Gum Tragacanth to regular fondant.

How to Make Modelling Paste

Throughout this book we refer to 'paste', meaning modelling paste. You can convert regular shop-bought fondant into modelling paste by adding CMC/Tylose powder, which is a thickening agent.

Add approx 1 tsp of CMC/Tylose powder to 225g (8oz) of fondant/sugarpaste. Knead well and leave in an airtight freezer bag for a couple of hours.

Add too much and it will crack. If this happens, add in a little shortening (white vegetable fat) to make it pliable again.

Tools

1 Foam Pad – holds pieces in place while drying.

2 Rolling pin – acrylic works better than wooden when working with fondant/paste.

3 Edible glue – essential when creating models. See below.

4 Rejuvenator spirit – mix with food colourings to create an edible paint.

5 Petal Dust, pink – for adding a 'blush' effect to cheeks.

6 Round and scalloped cutters – a modelling essential.

7 Piping nozzles – used to shape mouths and indents.

8 Shaped cutters – various uses.

9 Ball tool/serrated tool – another modelling essential.

10 Small pointed tool – used to create details like nostrils and holes.

11 Quilting tool – creates a stitched effect.

12 Veining tool – for adding details to flowers and models.

13 Craft knife/scalpel – everyday essential.

14 Brushes – to add finer details to faces.

15 Moulds – create detailed paste buttons, fairy wings and lots more.

16 Wooden skewers – to support larger models.

17 Spaghetti strands – also used for support.

18 Coated craft wire – often used in flower making.

Edible Glue

Whenever we refer to 'glue' in this book, we of course mean 'edible glue'. You can buy bottles of edible glue, which is strong and great for holding larger models together. You can also use a light brushing of water, some royal icing, or make your own edible glue by dissolving ¼ teaspoon tylose powder in 2 tablespoons warm water. Leave until dissolved and stir until smooth. This will keep for up to a week in the refrigerator.

Making Shoes

Throughout this book are some stunning shoe toppers in various sizes. These require a few pieces of fairly inexpensive specialist kit to make, are great fun, and look fantastic too!

These shoes use Florist paste instead of fondant/modelling paste, as it dries to a very hard consistency and allows the shoe to hold its shape well.

Large Shoes

The large leopard print shoe uses the *'Jem Ladies Shoe Cutter Set'*, which is widely available online. If you don't have this, we have provided similar templates to use on p48. You will also need a 4" heel mould, and a large 'drying ramp' – see photos – which holds the heel and sole together in place while the whole shoe structure dries hard.

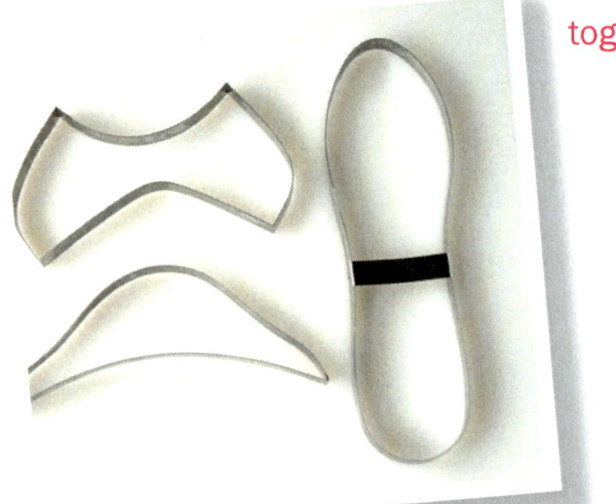

Medium Shoes

The beautiful bridal and floral shoes are medium sized and use the medium sized *'Jem Ladies Shoe Cutter Set'* – pictured. This set comes with heel moulds and drying ramps included.

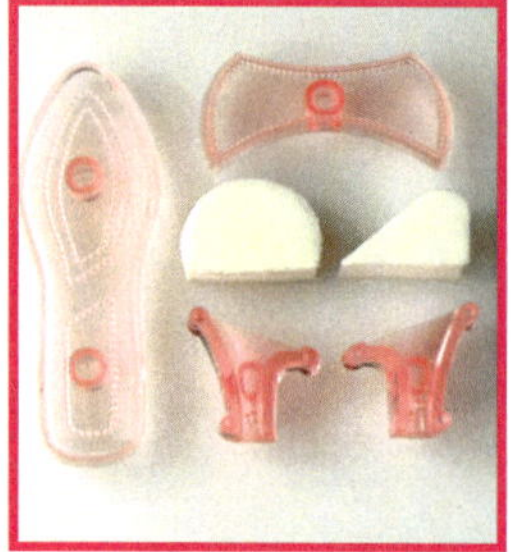

Mini Shoes

The super cute mini shoe cupcake toppers use the *Mini Shoe Cutter Set*, also from *Jem*, which is basically a tiny version of the other two designs. The mini shoes could be a great place to start if you have not made shoes before! You can make various styles by changing the decorative details, and make mules or add straps for a new shoe style!

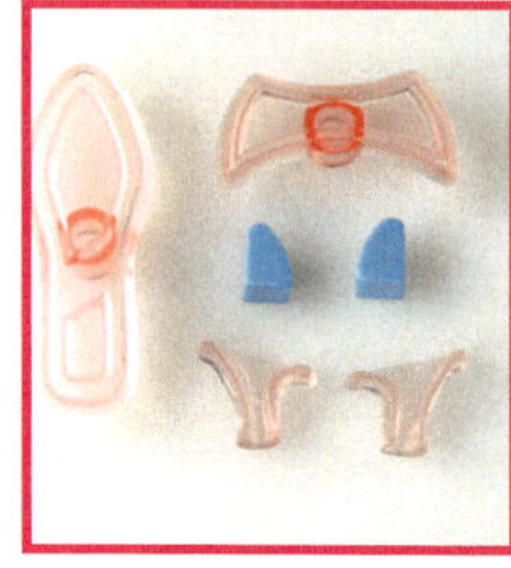

Cupcake Toppers

When making small figures for cupcakes, it's great to place each on a topper disc, and place this on top of a lovely swirl of buttercream. This way the figure can be removed and kept, and the child can tuck into the main cupcake.

Regular round cutters are essentials, and there are also a great selection of embossing tools and sheets out there that, when pressed into your rolled paste, will create cool quilting effects on your disc. Make your discs first and allow them to harden before you fix your figures to them.

You can also combine a scalloped cutter with the point of a small, round piping nozzle to create discs with cut-out holes.

Moulds and cutters are great ways to make special details for your toppers – the bridal shoe and bag in this book use this cute '*Roses Galore*' mould!

Painting Details

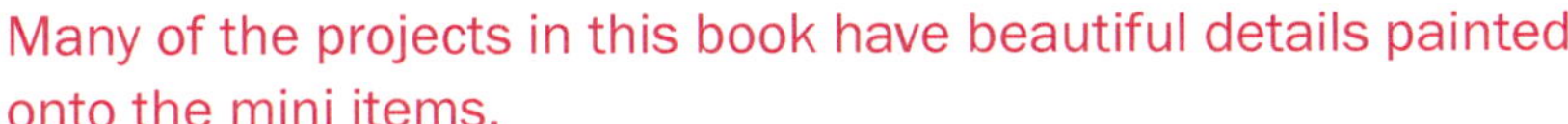

Many of the projects in this book have beautiful details painted onto the mini items.

Mixing regular gel or paste food colouring, or lustre dusts, with rejuvenator spirit will create edible paint in any colour you need. Keep a small collection of fine painbrushes handy too!

White paint – *Americolor Bright White* gel paste colour is strong enough to paint on clear white details.

Gold or Silver accents – mix lustre dust with rejuvenator spirit for an edible metallic finish.

Coloured details – mix your regular food colouring with rejuvenator spirit to create edible paint.

Shopaholic Cake

Materials

Modelling paste:
Flesh
Pink
Baby blue
Red
Yellow
White
Food colouring: white
Petal dust: pink
Rejuvenator spirit
Edible marker pens
Edible glue

Tools

Craft knife/scalpel
6" cake dummy
Bamboo skewer
Quilting tool
Veining tool
Cone tool
Paintbrush
Piping tip

1 First let's make our shopaholic girl!

2 Roll out a tapered sausage, and shape at the knee and ankle by rolling your little finger lightly over the parts you want to indent.

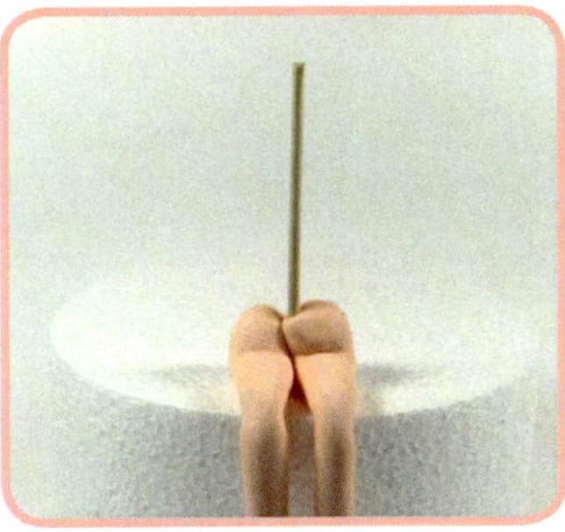

3 Arrange the legs on a cake dummy and place a skewer through the middle, going into the cake dummy about an inch of the way.

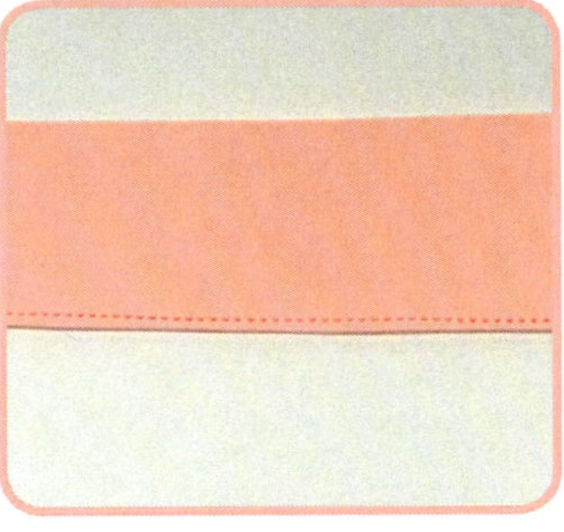

4 Cut out a rectangular piece of paste and stitch along the bottom edge with the quilting tool.

5 Gather the top edge of the rectangle, and arrange around the legs to form the skirt.

6 Roll out a cone shape for the torso and flatten it with your hand.

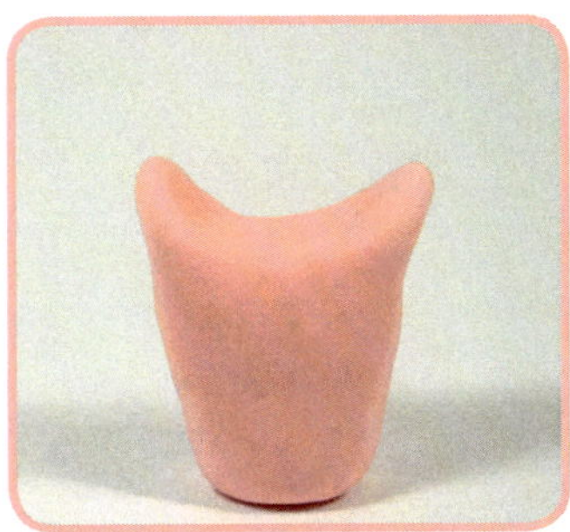

7 Shape the larger end to make the sleeves and neckline for the bodice.

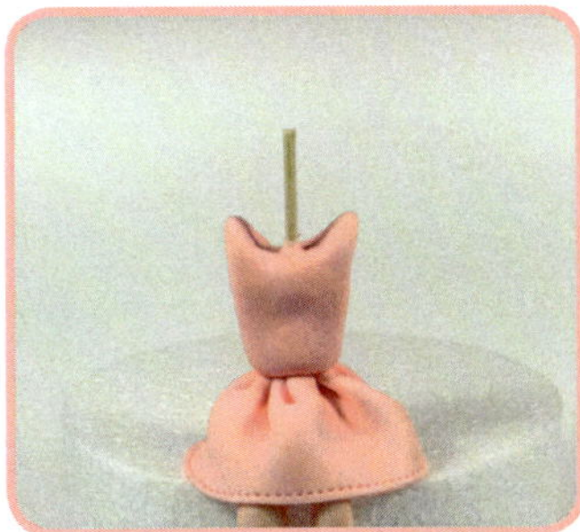

8 Insert this over the skewer and press firmly on to the legs.

9 Using a small amount of flesh coloured paste, fill in the neckline area.

10 Roll a smooth ball and add the head.

11 Add three tiny balls for the ears and nose. Use a cone tool to indent the ears.

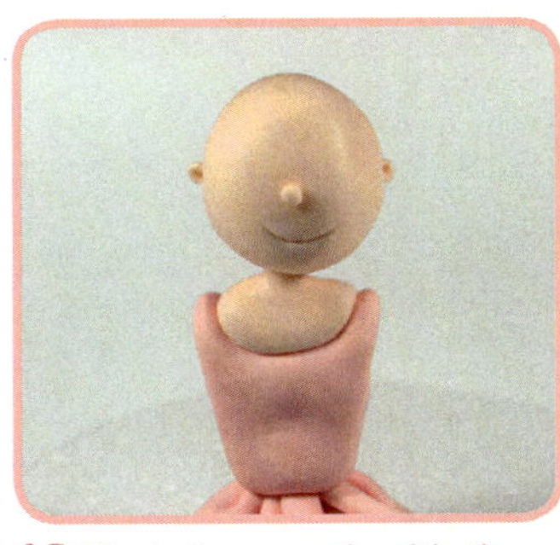

12 Mark the mouth with the end of a piping tip.

13 Open up the mouth, using a veining tool.

14 Add a tiny sausage of dark pink paste to fill in the mouth.

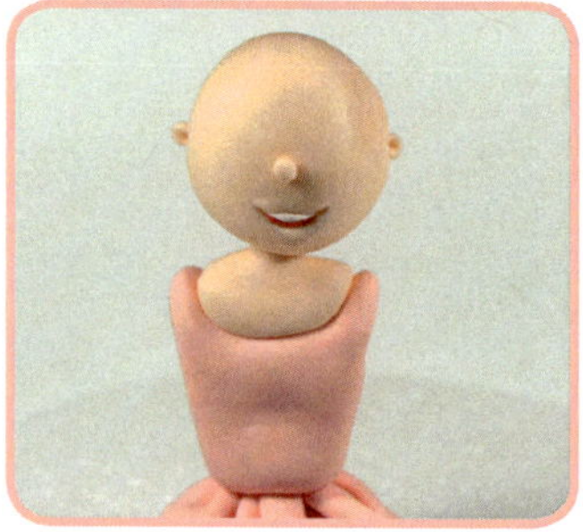

15 Add a tiny sausage of white paste to make the teeth.

16 Now for the sunglasses! Roll out two balls of brown paste.

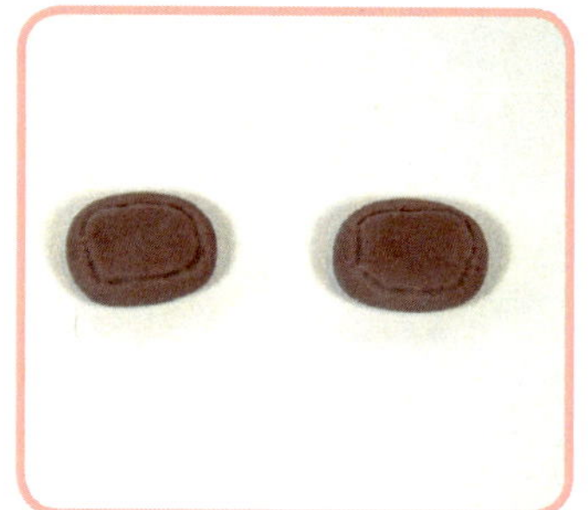

17 Flatten slightly, and mark the rims with a veining tool.

18 Make the bridge using a tapered sausage of paste.

19 Roll out two longer tapered sausages, and flatten the fatter ends.

20 Arrange the sunglasses and bridge on the front of the face. Glue in place.

21 Add the arms of the sunglasses.

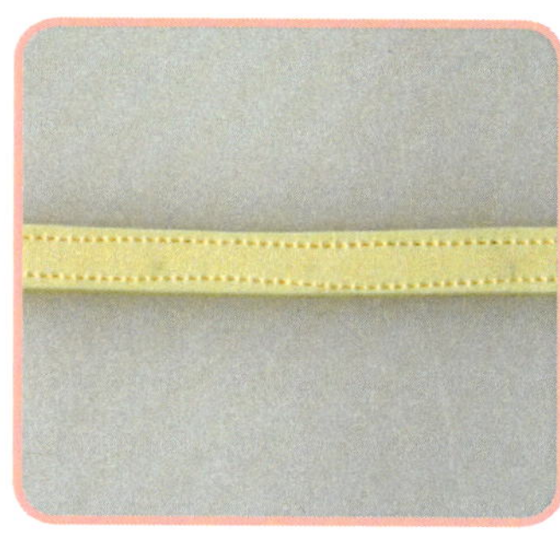

22 Roll out a long strip of paste, marking a stitched effect on each edge with the quilting tool.

23 Glue to the waist band to cover the joins, and also add a fine sausage of paste to the neckline.

24 Paint some polka dots on the dress.

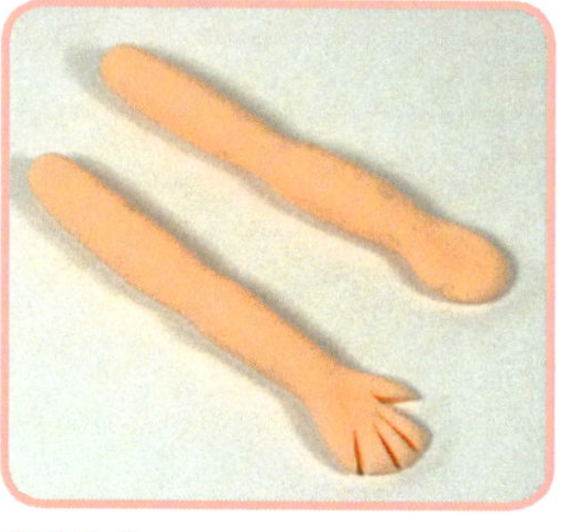

25 Roll out two sausages of paste, indenting at the elbow and wrist. Flatten the hand and make four cuts for the fingers.

26 Arrange and glue the arms onto your model.

27 Paint on some reflection details on the sunglasses using white food colouring.

28 With a dry brush and pink petal dust, add blush to the cheeks.

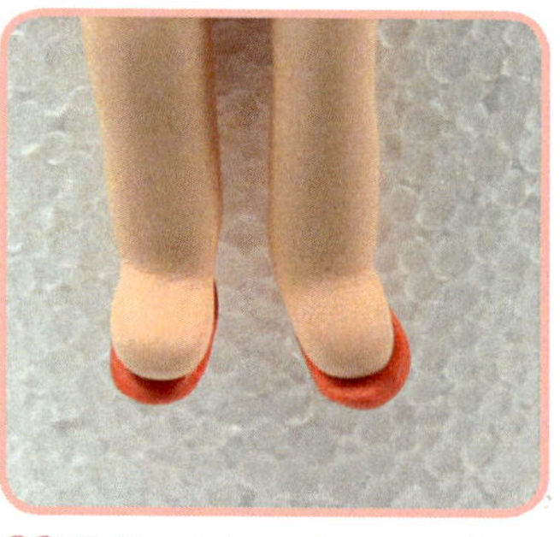

29 Roll out two elongated sausages, and flatten. Glue to the soles of the feet.

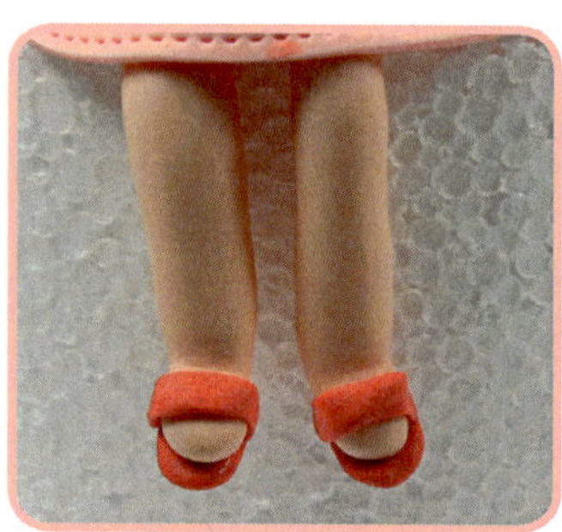

30 Roll out two narrow sausages, flatten, and glue over the top of the foot, to meet the sole at either side.

31 Roll out lots of sausages for the hair, and start to glue onto the head.

32 Keep going all the way around the head until the head is completely covered.

33 Add some finer sausages to cover any gaps, and some finer wisps for the fringe.

34 Now, just what has she been buying today?

35 Roll out a ball of paste and flatten.

36 Using your forefinger and thumb, pinch the paste at the top in the middle all the way through to create the handle, smoothing any bits away.

37 Add some scrunches to the bag with a veining tool.

38 Once the bag has dried, using the fine end of the marker pen write on your desired logo.

39 Some bags come with a rope handle...

40 Roll out a ball of paste, flattening and squaring it off until you have a square shape.

41 Using the veining tool, open up the top of the bag.

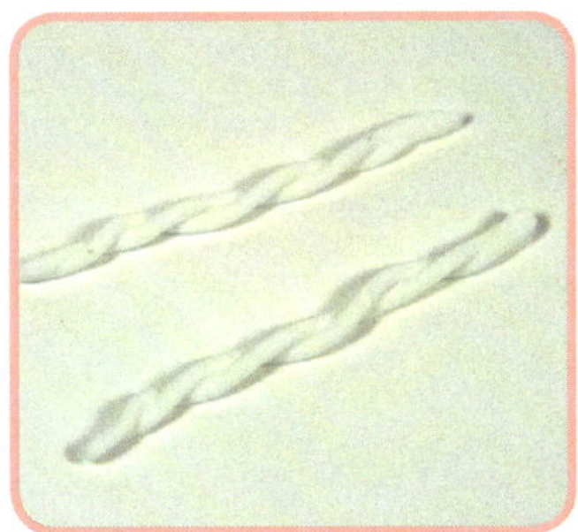

42 Make two long sausages and twist them together to make the handles.

43 Make four holes with the end of a paintbrush near the bag opening.

44 Attach the handles, securing with glue.

45 Once dried, draw or paint on your desired logo.

46 You can make as many bags as you require and have fun making your favourite shops!

Shopaholic Cupcakes
JIMMY CHOO
LONDON
SELFRIDGES & CO
GUCCI
$100
$100
$50
$100
$20

Materials

Modelling paste (for the accessories)
Florist paste (for the bags)
Edible marker pens
Edible glue

Tools

Craft knife/scalpel
Veining tool
Quilting tool
Fine paintbrush

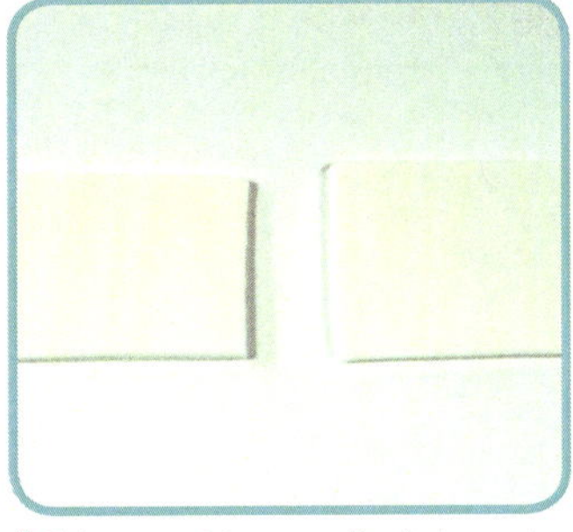

1 We need to use florist paste for the shop bags as it dries hard and holds the shape well. Cut two rectangles for front and back and leave to dry.

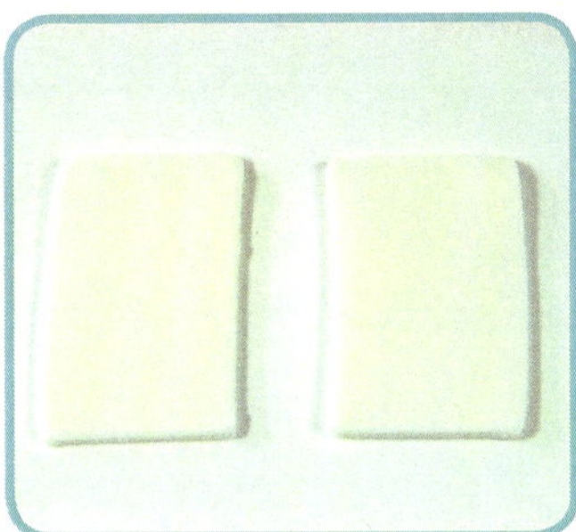

2 Cut a further two smaller rectangles of flower paste for the sides

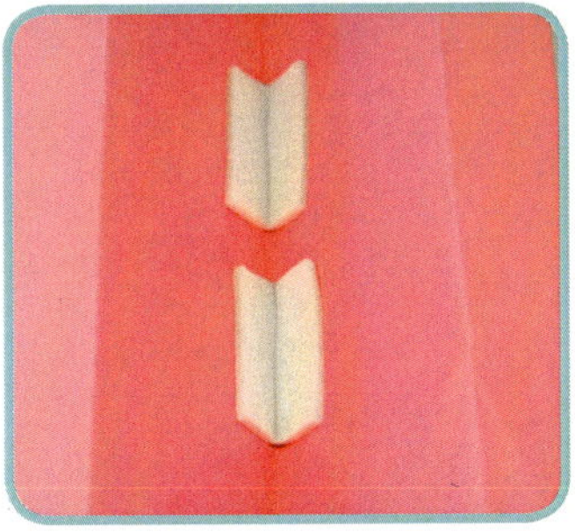

3 Using a folded piece of card as a support, make a line down the centre of each side rectangle, and leave them to dry in this position.

4 Once the pieces are dry, assemble the bag, securing with edible glue.

5 Roll two small sausages for the handles and attach.

6 Make as many bags as required, in different colours and logos! Draw on your desired logo using edible marker pens or edible paint.

7 To make the clutch bag, start by rolling out an oval of paste. You can use modelling OR florist paste for this.

8 Mark a criss cross pattern with the quilting tool and make indentations near the top with a veining tool.

9 To make the purse, flatten a ball of paste.

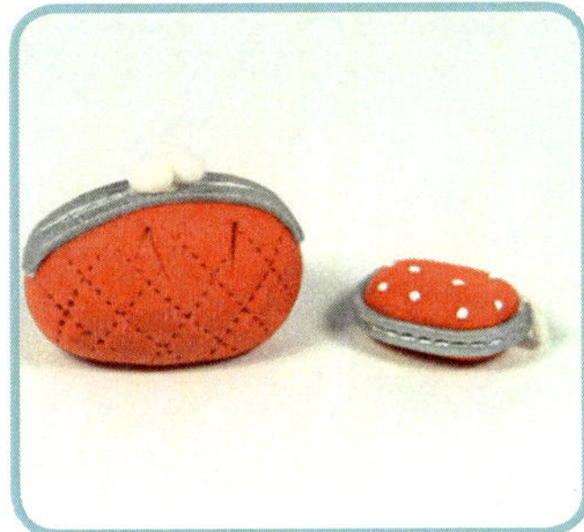

10 For final details, add a strip of paste around the top of the bag, a couple of balls for the clasp, and a stitched strip for the zip of the purse. Paint on the detail.

11 For the money, cut several small rectangles of paste with a craft knife and leave to dry.

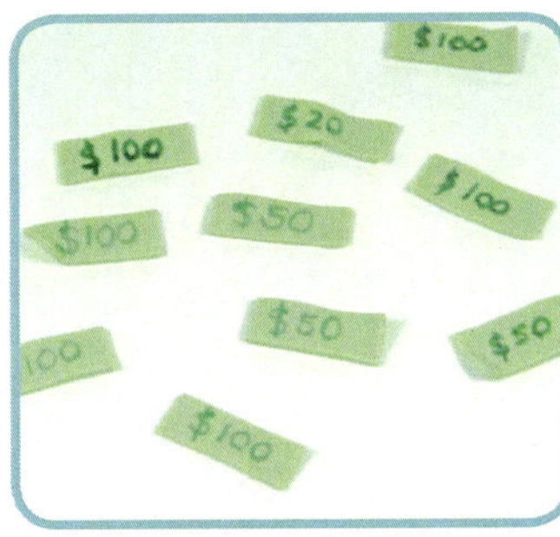

12 Paint on the money detail either with an edible marker, or food colouring.

13 To make the credit cards, cut out rounded edged rectangles with a craft knife in a few different colours.

14 Once dried, draw on the detail using edible marker pens.

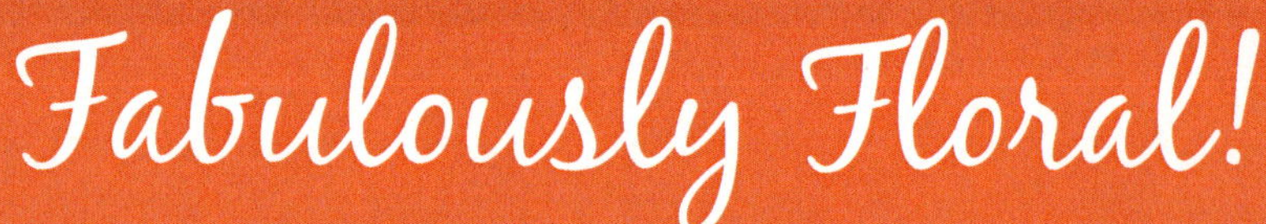
Fabulously Floral!

Materials

Florist Paste for shoe
Modelling paste:
Red
Pink
Green
White
Brown
Food color: pink, green, white
Lustre dust: silver
Rejuvenator spirit
Edible glue

Tools

Craft knife/ scalpel
Jem Ladies Shoe Cutter Set
Quilting tool
Veining tool
Pastry circle cutter: 58mm (2 ¼")
Heart cutter
Foam pad
Piping tip, No.4
Paintbrush

1 The shoe here uses the Jem Ladies Shoe Cutter set and florist paste as this dries harder than regular modelling paste.

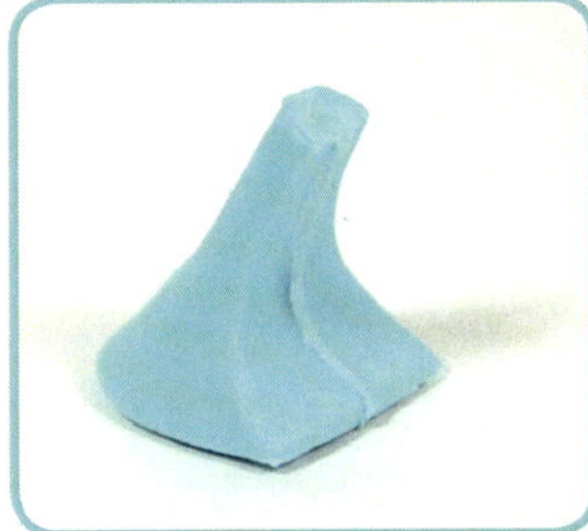

2 Make the heel using the mould, and turn upside down to dry. Leave it overnight to firm up.

3 Cut out a sole, flip it over to reveal the smooth side, and glue it to the heel. Leave it to dry over the foam drying ramp.

4 Cut out the lining sole in a light brown colour, and cut off the toe section.

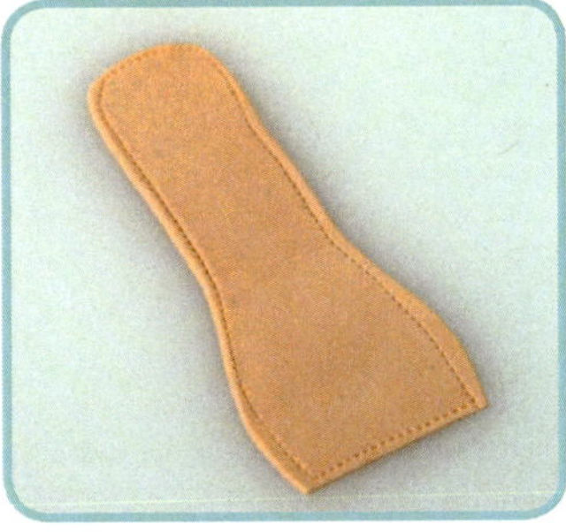

5 Stitch the detail using the quilting tool.

6 Glue the lining to the sole.

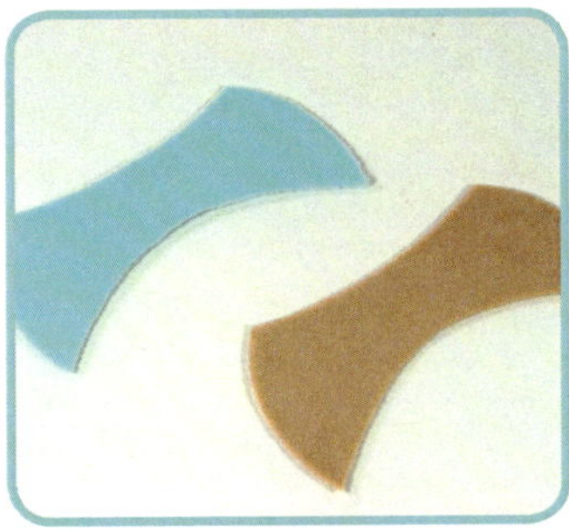

7 Cut out two identical toe section pieces.

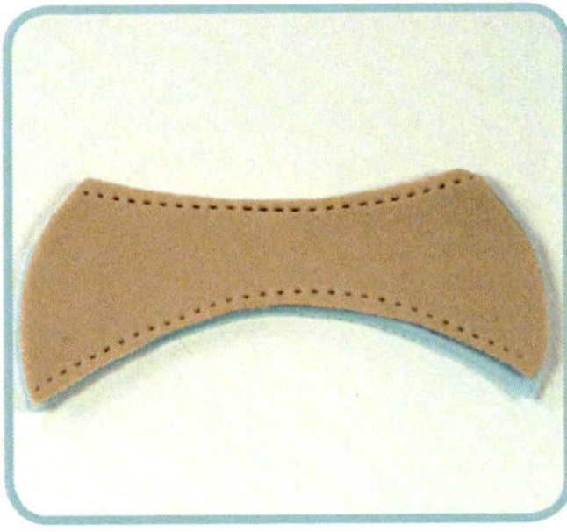

8 Glue them together, with the smooth side up, and stitch the lining with the quilting tool.

9 Attach the toe section to the sole, supporting it with the foam piece if required.

10 Cut out a circle of paste using a 58mm (2 ¼") pastry cutter

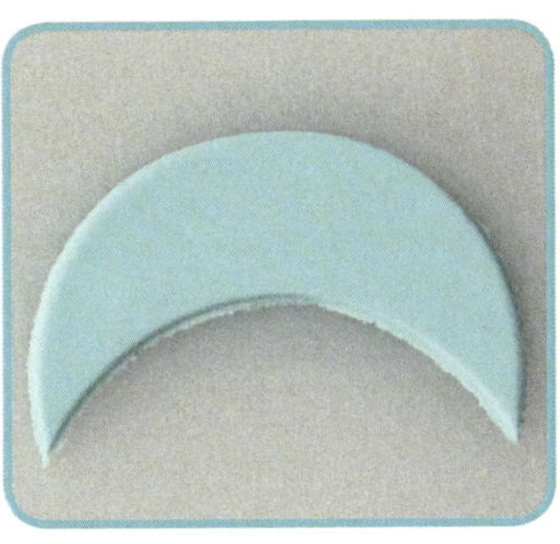

11 Using the same pastry cutter, remove just over half of the circle, as pictured.

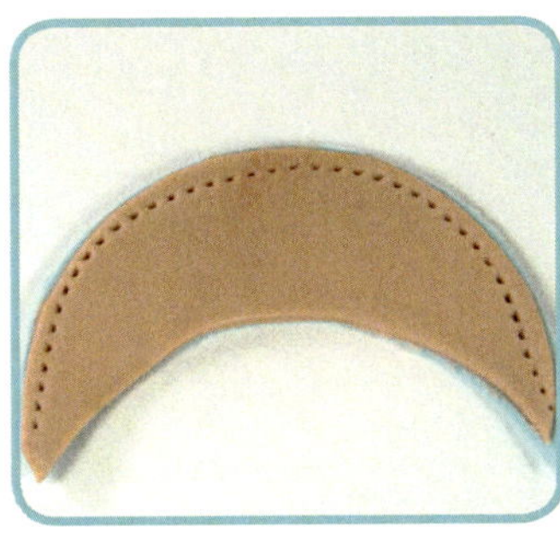

12 Cut out an identical piece for the lining, stick them together, and stitch the lining across the top edge.

13 Stick it to the back of the shoe, pinching ever so slightly at the top.

14 Roll out a long thin sausage of paste.

15 Attach it to the toe and heel section of the shoe.

16 Mix some pink and white food colour together to get a lighter shade. Paint some messy circles all over the shoe.

17 Using the pink neat, and painting in a circular motion, lightly paint the rose detail.

18 Paint on some green leaf details.

19 Using the green neat, add a little bit of detail to the leaves. It doesn't have to look perfect!

20 Add a few polka dots inbetween the flowers with some white food colouring.

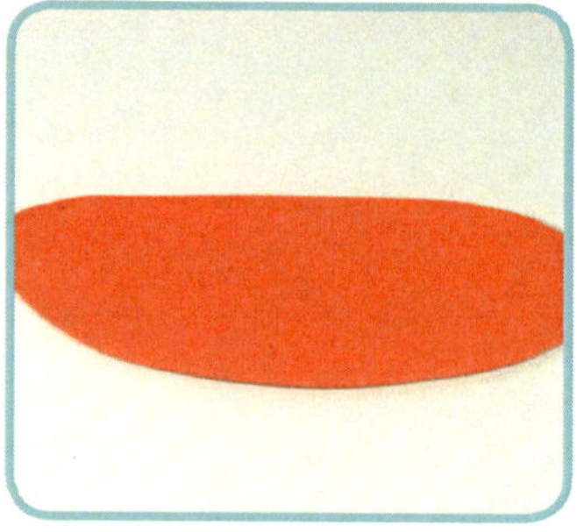
21 Roll out a sausage, and flatten it with a rolling pin.

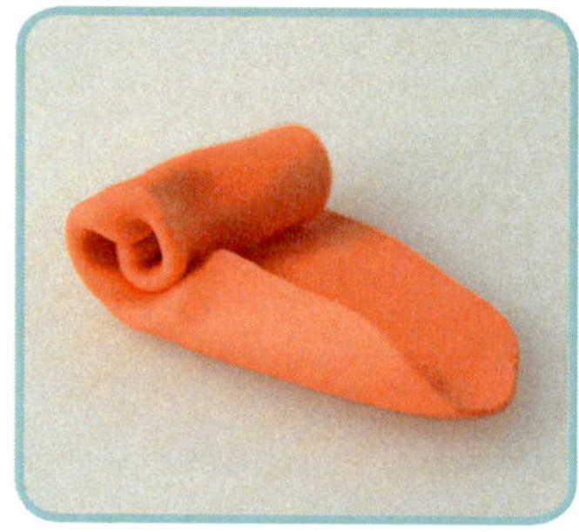
22 Roll over the top edge, and start to spiral the sausage of paste in to a rose shape.

23 Once all rolled up, pinch it at the bottom to secure.

24 Cut off the excess paste so it lies flat on a surface.

25 Roll out two green tear-drop shapes for the leaves and flatten.

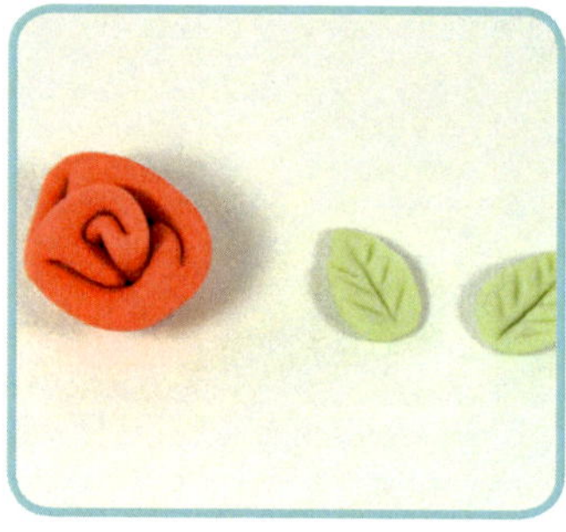
26 Mark on some leaf detail with a veining tool.

27 Attach the leaves and rose to the top of the shoe

28 Cut out a little heart for the label inside the shoe, and paint on some little polka dots with white food colouring.

29 And now for the matching handbag!

30 Roll out a large ball of paste, flatten it with the heel of your hand. Pinch up the sides to shape the bag.

31 Cut out two rectangles of paste and attach to the sides of the bag. Also mark on some scrunches in the bag with a veining tool.

32 Cut a strip of paste, and stitch it up the middle. Cut out a triangle shape for the zipper pull, cutting off the top point, and remove a little triangle in the centre.

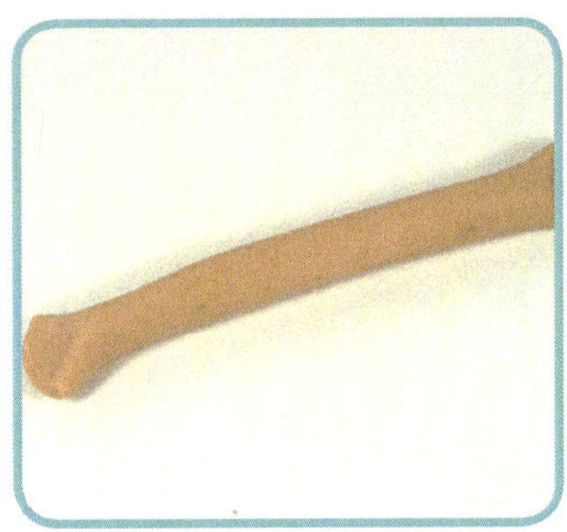

33 Roll out two sausages of paste, flattening at both ends

34 Glue both of the sausages on to the bag to make the handles.

35 Using a no. 4 piping tip, mark the rivet details on the handles. Roll out a fine sausage of white paste and attach to the edges of the bag.

36 Paint the zip with silver lustre dust.

37 Paint little polka dots all over the bag using white food colouring.

38 Matching red lipstick!

39 Roll out a little cylinder of black paste.

40 Roll out a sausage of red paste, and cut off the bottom to make it stand up.

41 Taper the end of the rounded end to look like a new lipstick.

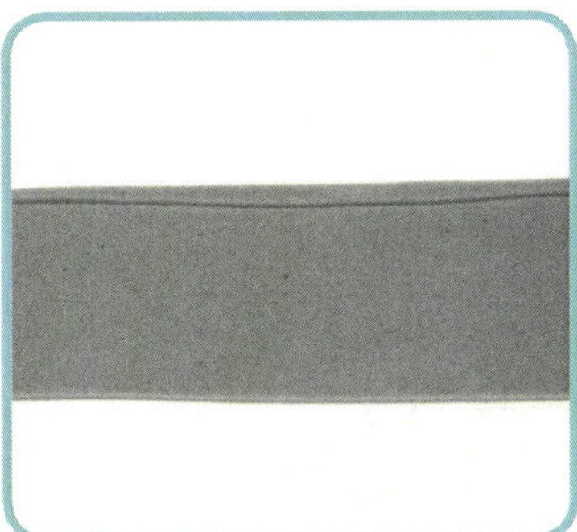

42 Cut out a rectangle of paste, and with the cutting wheel, mark the edge with a continuous line, being careful not to cut through the paste.

43 Wrap it around the lipstick, and trim at the bottom, securing it all with glue.

44 Stick this on to the black cylinder.

45 Make another sausage of black paste, cutting it straight at the bottom so it will stand up.

46 Paint the shaft of the lipstick with silver lustre dust.

Bridal Bag & Shoe

Materials

- Florist paste (for the shoe): white, pink
- Modelling paste (for the bag): white, pink
- Lustre dust: pearl ivory, silver
- Rejevenator spirit
- Edible pearls
- Non pareils
- Edible glue

Tools

- Craft knife/scalpel
- Jem Ladies Shoe Cutter Set
- Heart cutter
- Quilting tool
- First Impressions Roses Galore Mould
- 18 gauge florist wire
- Paintbrush

1 The shoe uses florist paste, as it dries firmer than modelling paste, and the Jem Ladies Shoe Cutter Set.

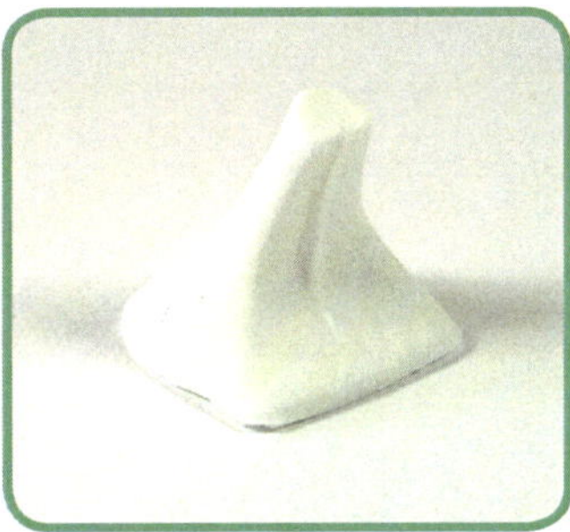

2 Grease the heel mould well and insert the paste to make the heel. Leave it upside down to dry overnight.

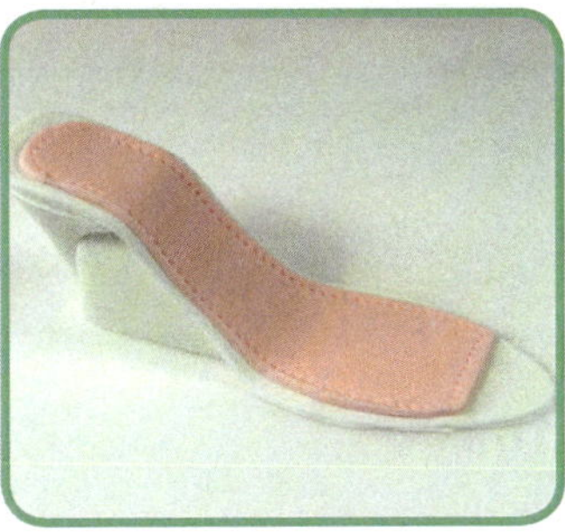

3 Cut out the sole to match the heel colour. Cut out another sole, and trim to fit over the top so it fits inside. Stitch the outer edge and cut off the toe section.

4 Cut out the back strap and toe section, securing with edible glue. Leave to dry before decorating.

5 Make some roses using the mould, trimming them to fit the toe section.

6 Decorate the shoe with the roses, gluing in place and filling in any gaps with edible pearls and non pareils.

7 Cut out a little heart to make the label.

8 Now for a beautiful matching handbag!

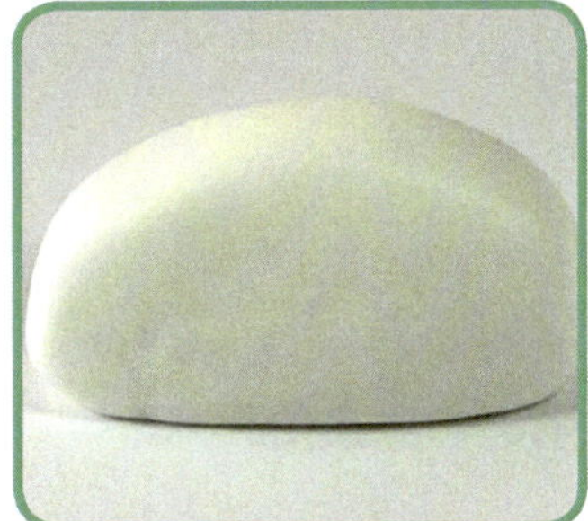

9 Roll out an oval ball of paste, flatten and then shape into a clutch bag shape.

10 Run the quilting tool diagonally across the front of the bag, and then again in the other direction to create the quilted effect.

11 Cut a strip of paste for the opening of the bag, marking a line down the centre of the strip. Roll two small balls for the clasp.

12 Cut a small piece of wire, and thread small flattened balls of paste to create the handle, leaving a little of the wire exposed at either end.

13 Insert the handle into the bag.

14 Paint with the silver lustre dust, and use a rose from the mould as before.

Leopard Skin Shoe

Materials

Florist paste:
Pale pink
Pink
Black
Tan
White
Food colouring: Dark brown, chestnut
Rejuvenator spirit
Edible pen: black
Edible glue

Tools

Craft knife/scalpel
Cake Structure 4" heel mould
Petal Crafts large drying ramp
Templates for the shoe
Quilting tool
Foam pad
Paintbrush

1 The shoe uses florist paste, as it dries firmer than modelling paste, and the templates from p.48 plus a 4" heel mould.

2 Roll out a large cone of florist paste for the heel.

3 Spread a fine layer of white vegetable fat/ shortening inside the mould so that the paste doesn't stick.

4 Press the paste into the mould.

5 Roll over it with a rolling pin.

6 Remove any excess.

7 Pop the mould in the fridge for 10 minutes, and the heel should release very easily.

8 Cut the tip off the heel and leave to dry for at least 24 hours, smooth side down on a foam pad.

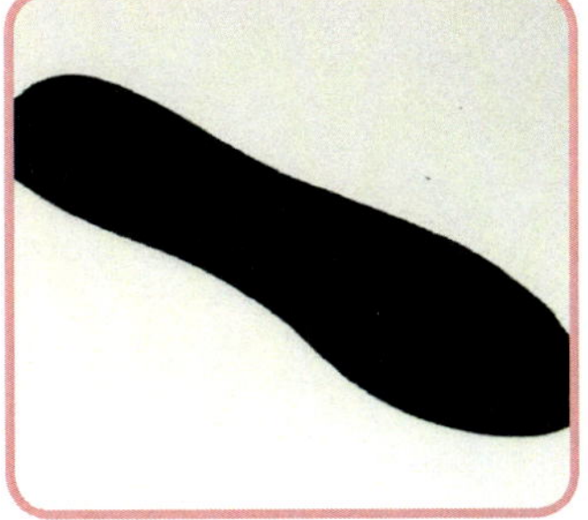

9 Cut out the sole shape using the templates.

10 Attach the sole to the heel, and place over the large rack, making sure the heel is in the correct position. Place the shoe on a foam pad as you work.

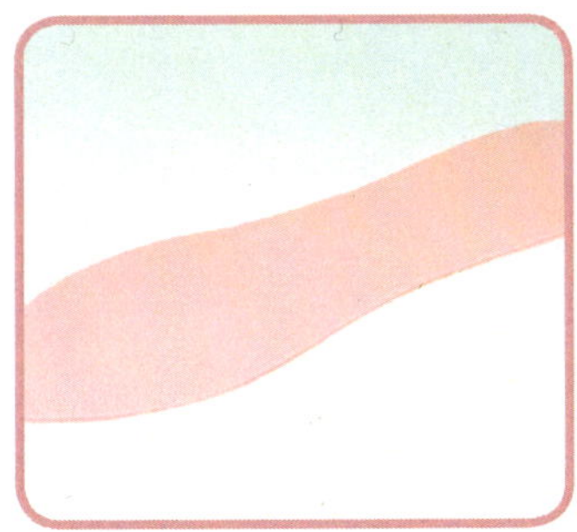

11 Cut out a contrasting colour for the lining of the sole.

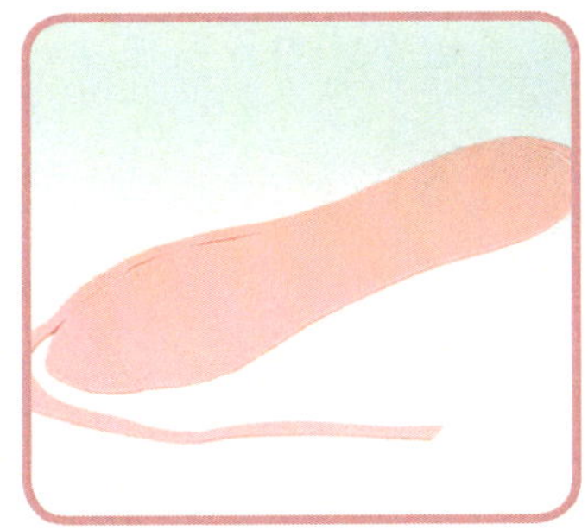

12 With a craft knife, cut away about 2mm all around the edge of the sole.

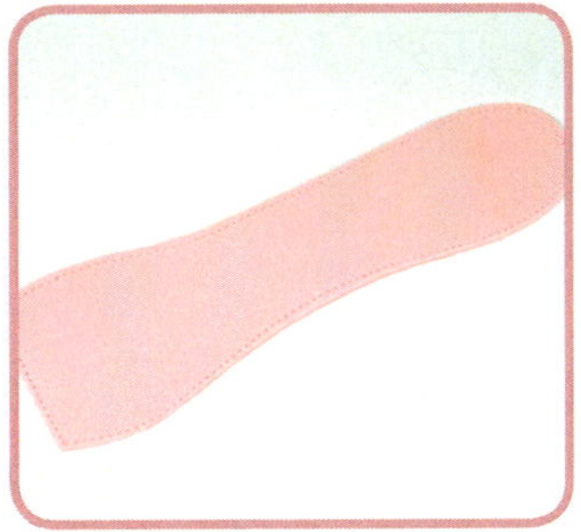

13 Cut away the toe section, and with the quilting tool, mark the detail.

14 Glue the lining on to the sole.

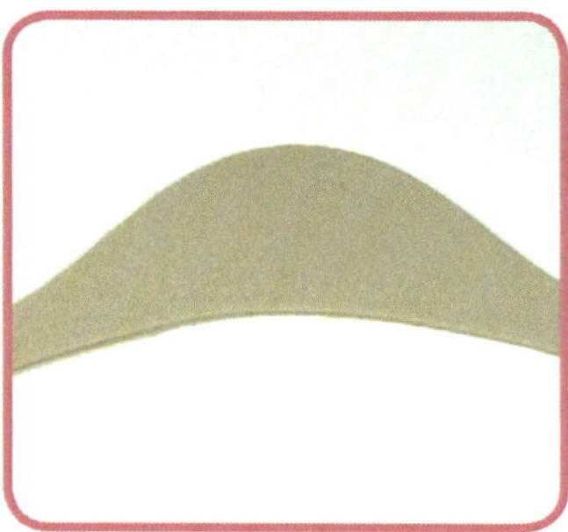

15 Cut out the back of the shoe using the template..

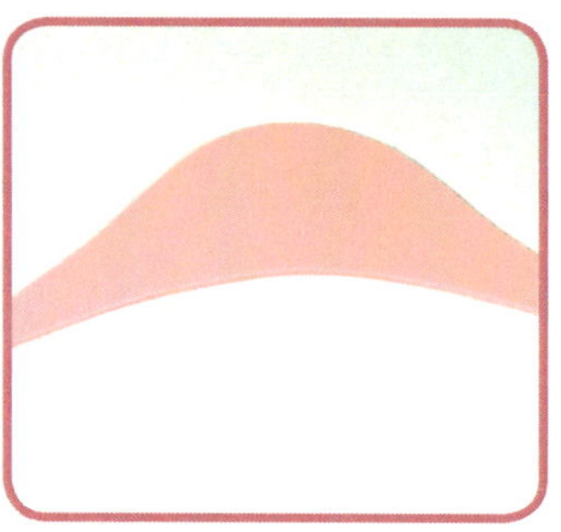

16 Cut out an identical piece for the heel section.

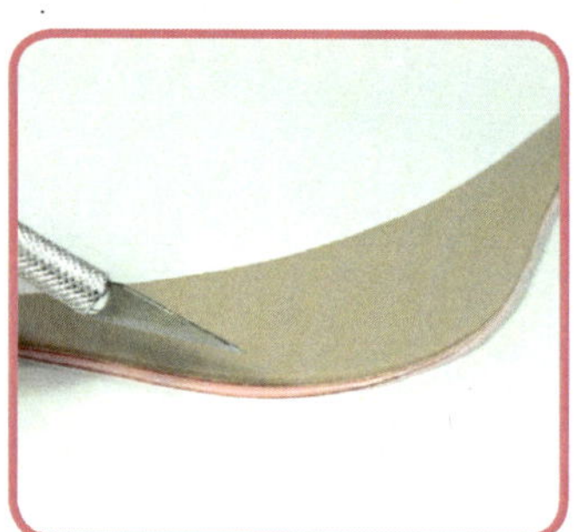

17 Glue them together and trim any excess off.

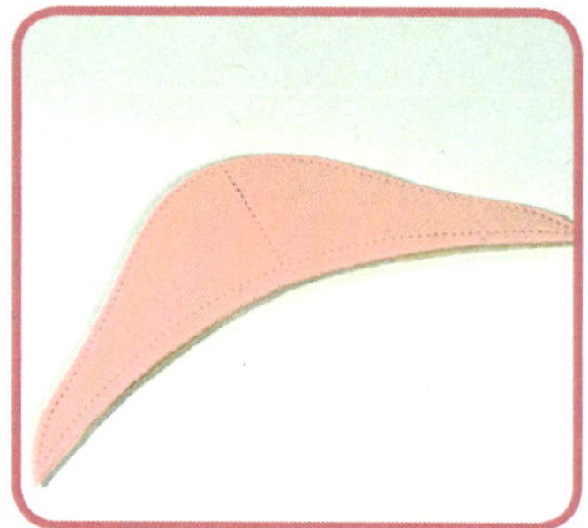

18 Mark the edges, and also up the centre, with the quilting tool.

19 Attach to the shoe, pinching the paste at the middle slightly.

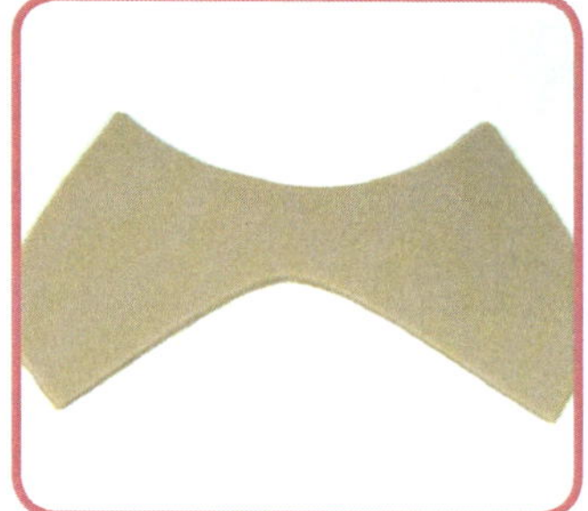

20 Cut out the toe section using the template.

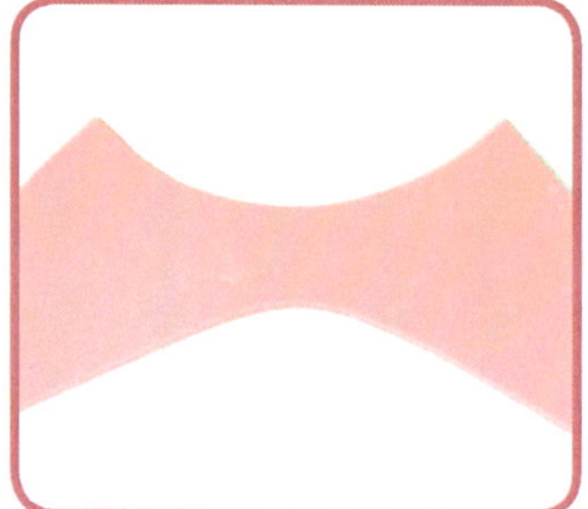

21 Cut out an identical piece in a contrasting colour.

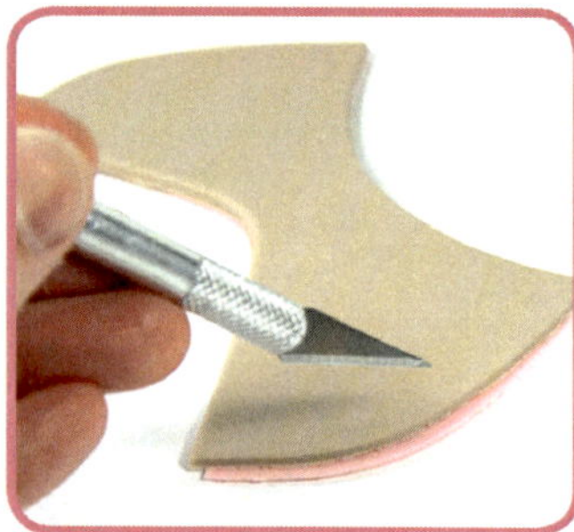

22 Trim if necessary.

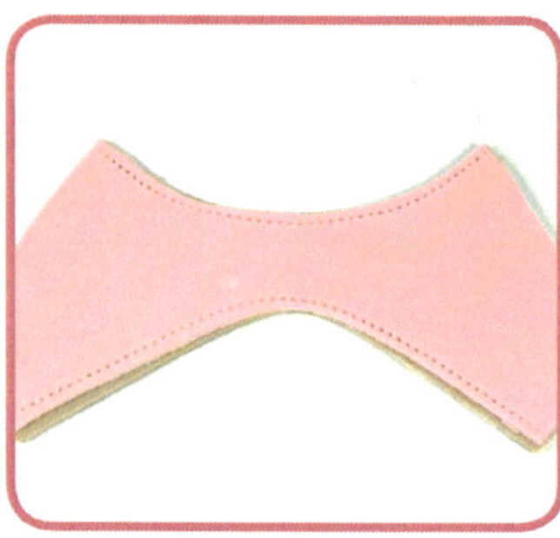

23 Mark both edges with the quilting tool.

24 Attach the toe section to the shoe, using a little kitchen towel (if necessary) to support it while it is drying.

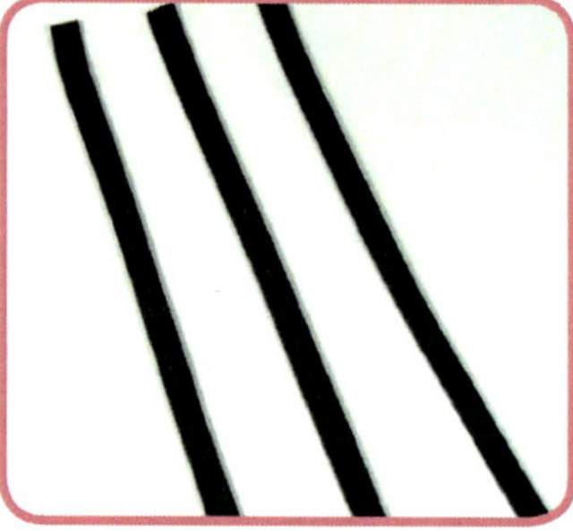

25 Cut out long strips of paste, and run the quilting tool along one edge.

26 Attach to each edge of the toe section.

27 Attach along the edge of the heel section.

28 Using the chestnut food colour, paint random blobs of colour on the shoe. They do not have to be even.

29 With the dark brown food colour, paint around the edges of the spots, but not all the way round. Add smudges of the brown in between the spots

30 Cut out a rectangle of paste, folding in the centre to make a mark.

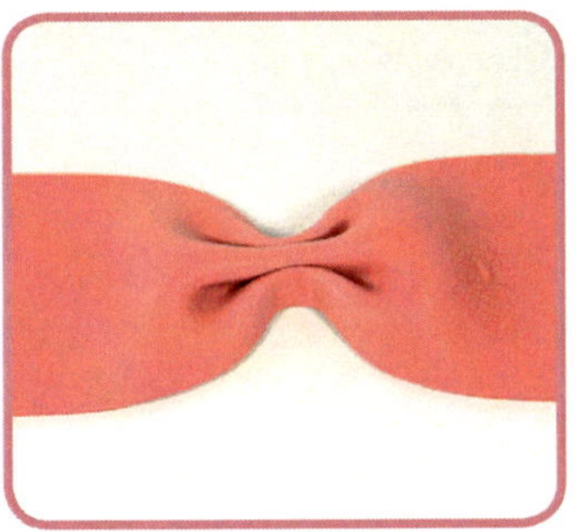

31 Gather it in the middle.

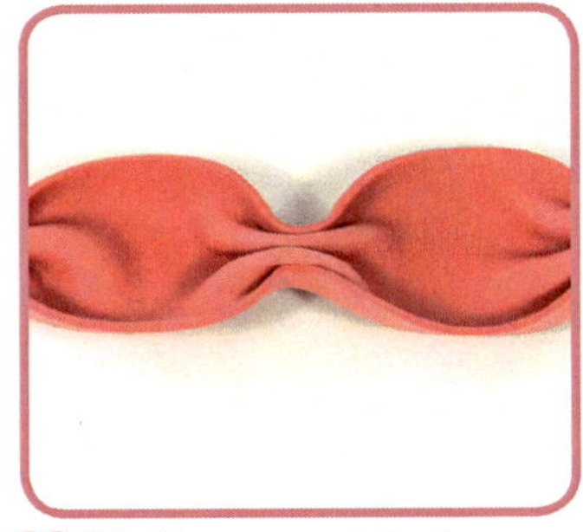

32 Flip it over, and do the same to both of the edges.

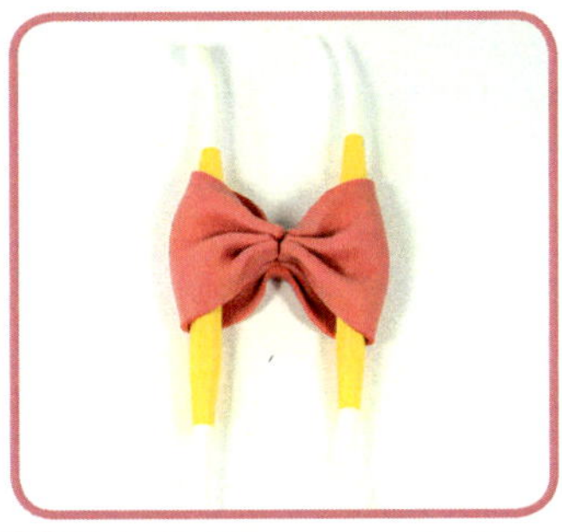

33 Using either some modelling tools, or paintbrushes to support the bow loops, bring both sides to the centre, securing with glue.

34 Cut out a long rectangle.

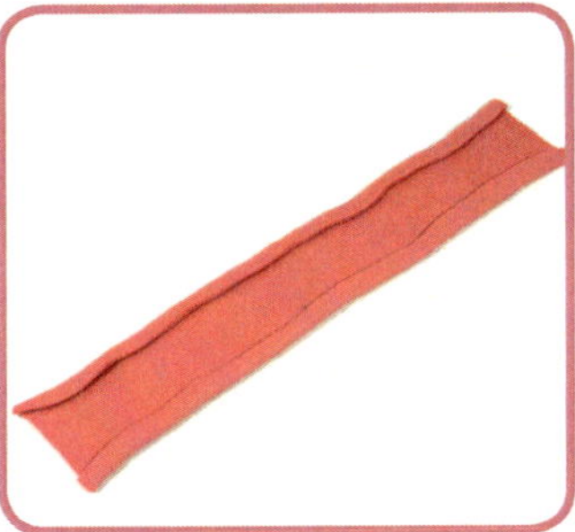

35 Turn over the edges..

36 Using a toothpick, place it under the paste, and pinch it over the top to make an indentation. Do this in a couple of places.

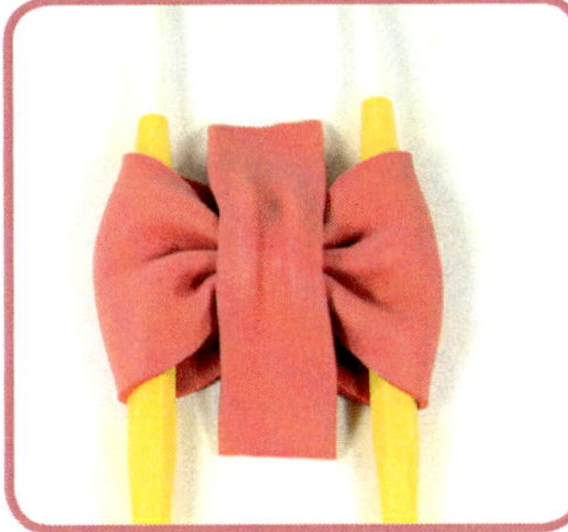

37 Lay the strip over the centre of the bow.

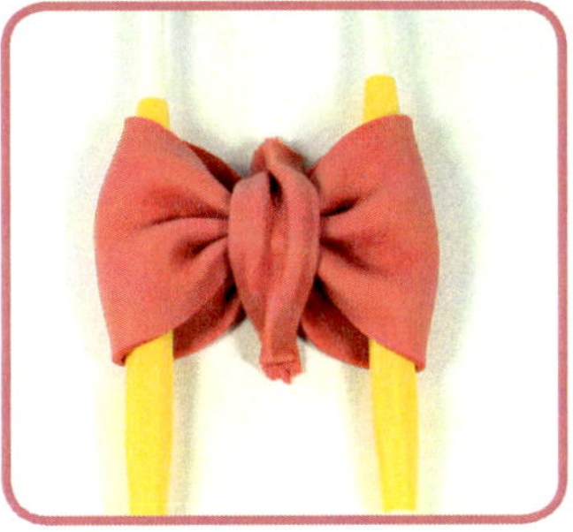

38 Cut the length of the paste to just fit neatly around the bow and pinch both edges.

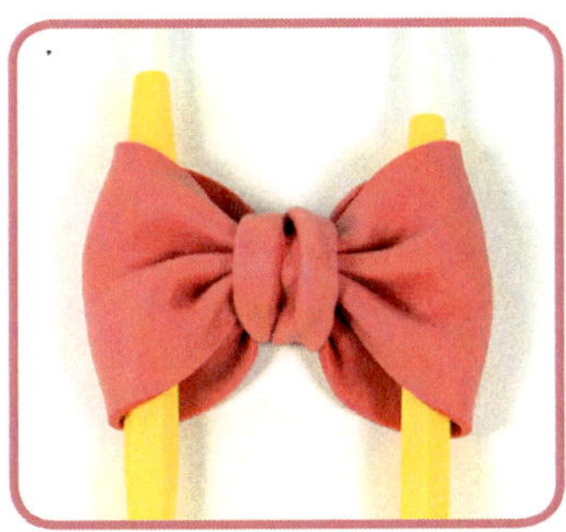

39 Secure at the back with a little glue.

40 Once dry, attach the bow to the shoe with edible glue.

41 Roll out some paste and attach it to the inner heel, trimming with a craft knife.

42 Cut a very fine strip of paste.

43 Attach it to the bottom of the heel.

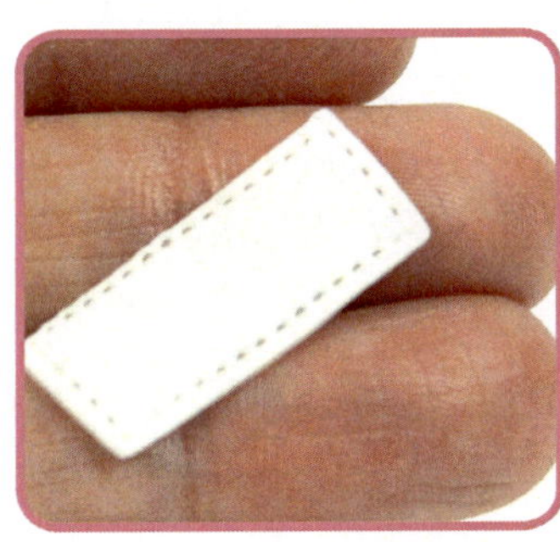

44 Cut out a small rectangle of white paste, stitching it around the edges.

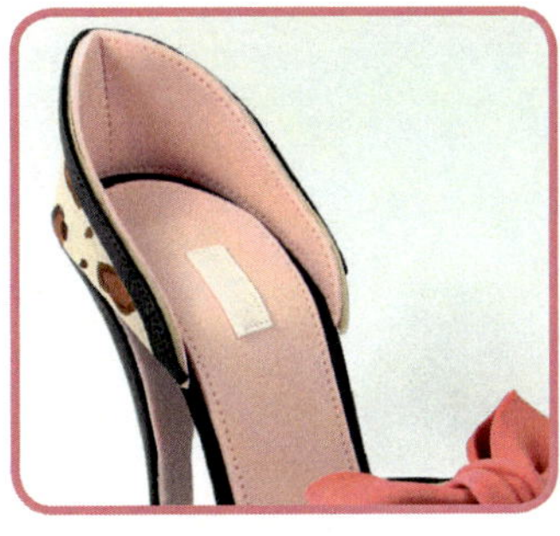

45 Stick it inside the shoe with some glue.

46 Using an edible marker, write a message, or your desired logo on it.

Leopard Skin Cupcakes

Materials

Florist Paste:
- Black
- Light pink
- Dark pink
- Tan

Food colouring:
- Pink
- Dark brown
- Chestnut
- Rejuvenator spirit
- Edible glue

Tools

- Craft knife/scalpel
- Jem mini shoe cutter
- Quilting tool
- Ball tool
- Teardrop cutter
- Blossom cutter
- Cake smoother
- Circle cutters
- Piping tip (size 4)
- Foam pad
- Paintbrush

1 The mini shoes use florist paste, because it dries firmer, and the Jem Mini Shoe cutter set. You can use regular modelling paste for the bags.

2 Lightly coat the heel mould with vegetable fat/shortening, and make the heel. Place upside down to dry for around 2 hours.

3 Cut out the sole, flipping it over to use the smooth side.

4 Attach the sole to the heel, supporting it (if necessary) with the included foam heel supports.

5 Using a tear drop cutter, make the lining for the shoe.

6 Cut out the top shoe section, flipping it over to use the smooth side. Glue to the sole.

7 Using the heel strap cutter, cut and attach two heel straps.

8 Paint on the leopard print (shown in detail on the large shoe tutorial) using a fine paintbrush.

9 Roll a ball of paste, and lots of tiny balls to make the jewels, and attach glue in place.

10 Attach the shoes to a disc of sugarpaste.

11 Now for a different style – a slip-on mule with bow detail!

12 Please follow steps 3-5.

13 Cut out the toe section, and attach to the sole.

14 Cut out the shape pictured, using a craft knife.

15 Concertina one end, and place into the centre of the bow, repeating for the other side.

16 Cut a small strip to cover the centre of the bow, securing at the back.

17 Paint on the leopard print detail.

18 Glue the bows on to the front of the shoes.

19 Place the shoes on to a disc of sugarpaste.

20 Here is another cute style!

21 Follow steps 3-5.

22 Cut out the toe section and attach to the sole.

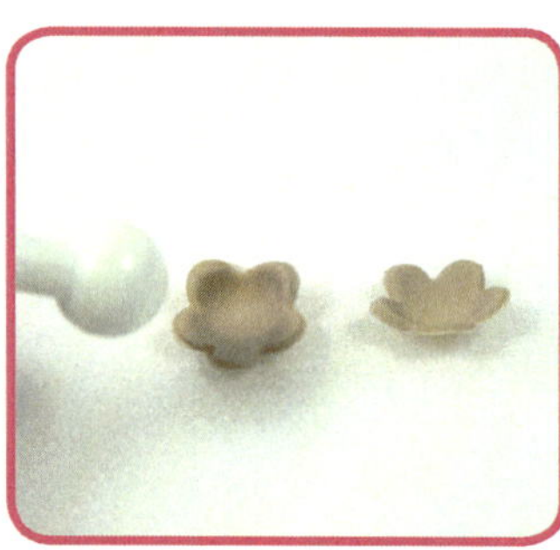

23 Cut out two blossoms and cup them by rolling the ball tool gently around the centre.

24 Place the blossoms on to the shoes, placing a little ball of paste for the centre.

25 Paint on the leopard detail and place on a disc of sugarpaste.

26 Let's make some matching mini bags!

27 Roll a ball of paste, squashing it slightly and squaring off the corners with either your hands or a cake smoother.

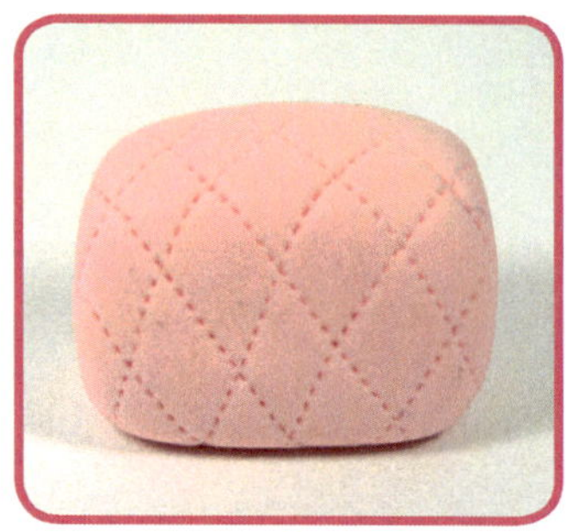

28 Mark the diagonal lines with the quilting tool.

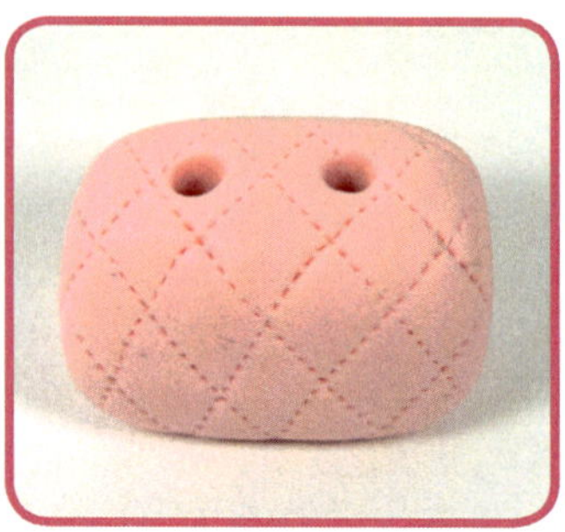

29 Make two holes on the top of the bag with the end of a paintbrush.

30 Attach a fine sausage of paste to make the piped edges, and a ball of paste to make the fastening.

31 Roll a sausage of paste and twist both ends together. Insert both ends in to the holes at the top of the bag, securing with glue.

32 Place the bag on a disc of sugarpaste.

33 Cute clutch!

34 Roll out a ball of paste, flattening slightly to make this shape.

35 Cut out a piece of paste in the above shape using a craft knife.

36 Stitch around the edges.

37 Secure the flap to the top of the bag, and make the jewel as before.

38 Paint on the leopard detail as before...

39...and place on a cupcake topper disc.

40 One more style to try!

41 Roll out a ball of paste, flattening it slightly. Square off both ends, and taper it at the top.

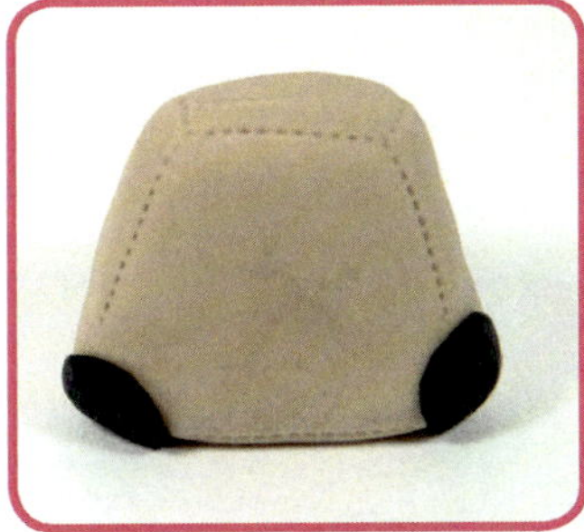

42 Cut out two circles of paste and place at the bottom corners of the bag, and mark some stitching detail.

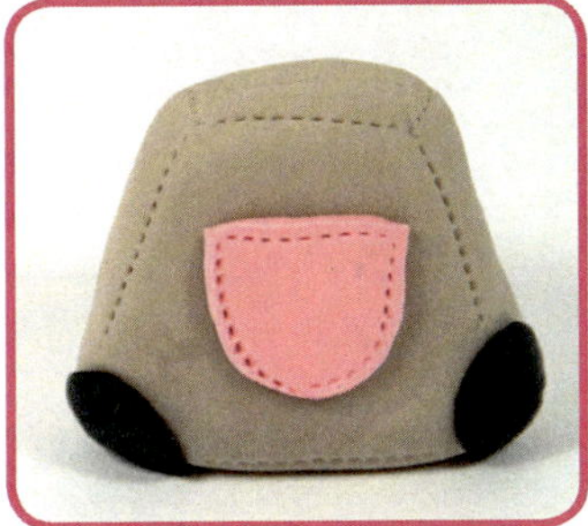

43 Cut out a pocket shape using the craft knife, and stitch around the edges. Using the piping tip, indent the rivet details.

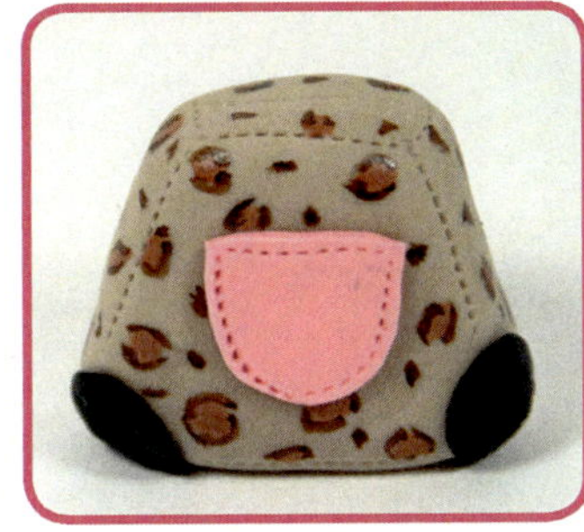

44 Paint on the leopard detail.

45 Cut out a strip of paste and attach to the top of the bag for the handle.

46 Place the bag on a cupcake topper disc.

Teen Queen Cake

Materials

- Fondant covered rectangular cake
- Modelling paste: White, Red, Blue, Pink, Yellow, Paprika, Black
- Edible paint: silver
- Petal dust: pink
- White non-pareils
- Edible glue

Tools

- Craft knife/scalpel
- Cake dummy
- Veining tool
- Cone tool
- Scallop tool
- Small ball tool
- Blossom cutters
- Small circle cutter
- Tiny heart cutter
- Wooden skewer/tooth-picks
- Paintbrushes

1 Start with a rectangular cake which will form the basis of your bed design. Keep the edges rounded to create a softer look.

2 Cake drums come in all shapes and sizes so choose your size based on whether you want cupcakes around your cake or simply on its own.

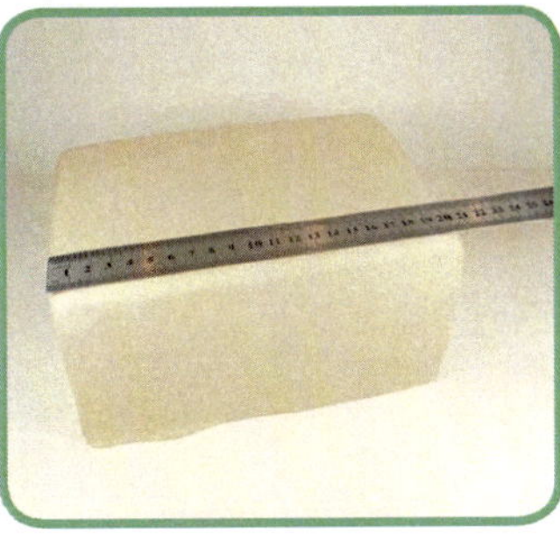

3 If you're not confident gauging the bedcover size by eye, measure your cake first by its length...

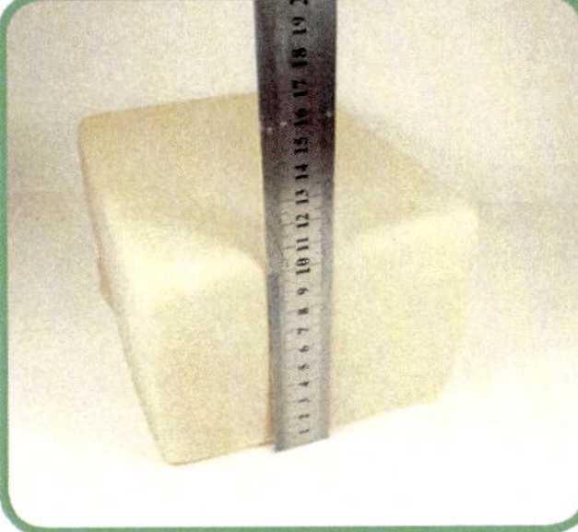

4 ...and then by its height. Add these together - length + height. Do the same using width + height.

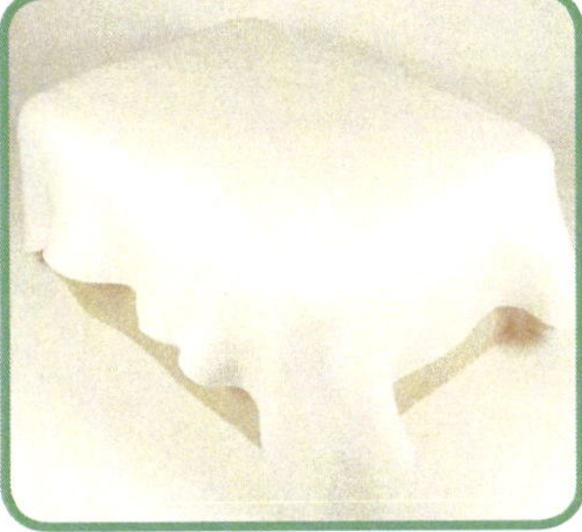

5 This will be the dimensions of the piece of paste to cut for your bedcover. Drape this over your 'bed', arranging into natural folds.

6 Add cute details, like these blossom shapes, from thinly rolled paste.

7 ...and further brightness with yellow flower centres.

8 Little hearts have been added here too!

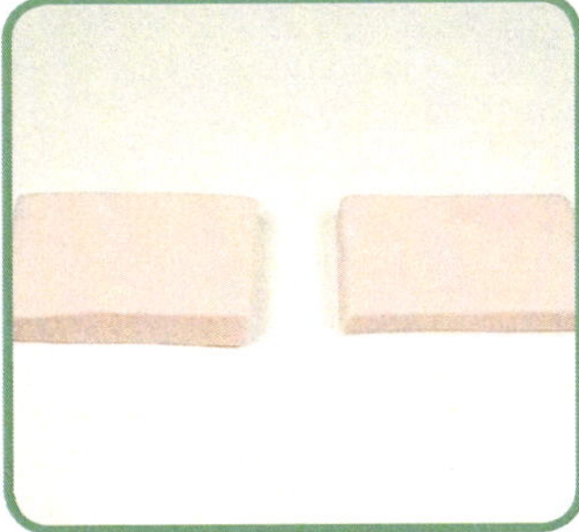

9 To make pillows, cut two deep pieces of paste (measure these against your bed design for accuracy).

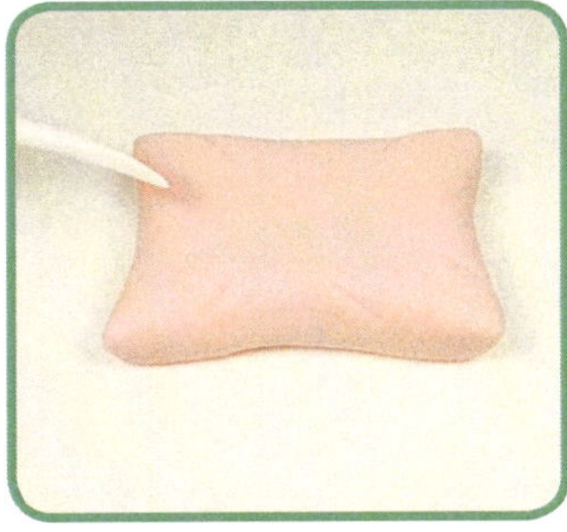

10 Gently shape the pillows with the pads of your fingers and add creases with your veining tool.

11 Instead of a headboard, you can add two simple bolsters by rolling thick sausages of paste.

12 The bolsters will help to raise your pillows up!

13 Create two further pillows to match the bedding, as before.

14 Add these to your design to complete a pretty look.

15 Every teenage bedroom needs a 'Teen Queen'!

16 Create the legs by rolling two sausages of paste and 'hollowing' the bottom using a cone tool.

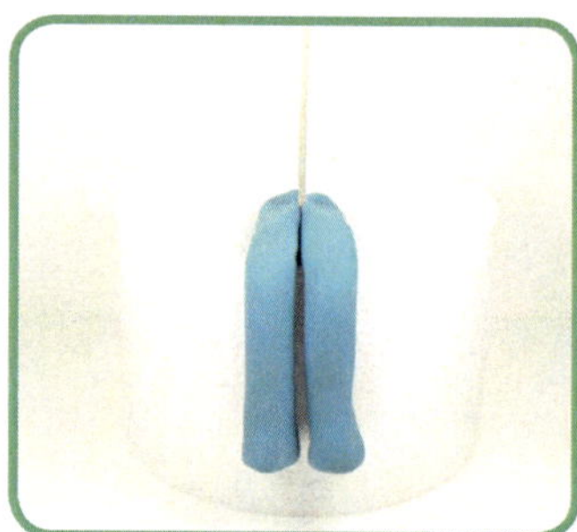

17 Insert a wooden skewer into a cake dummy for support and add the legs to this.

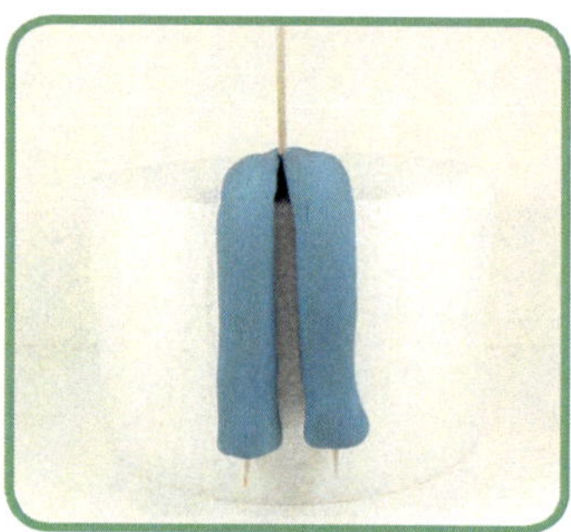

18 Insert two toothpicks into the bottoms of the legs.

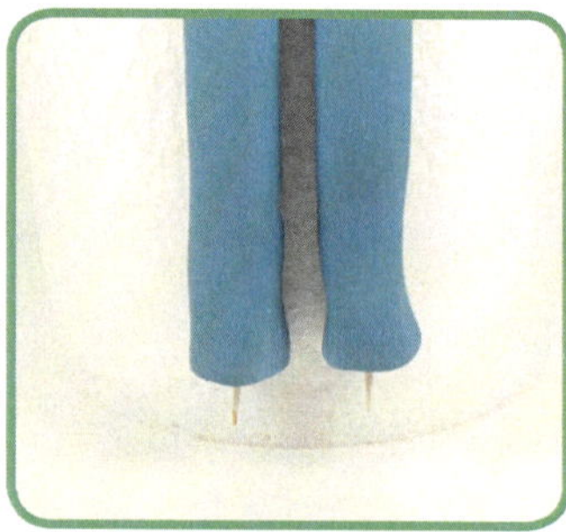

19 Leave just enough to take the feet/shoes for your figure.

20 Create a cone/teardrop shape of coloured paste.

21 Shape this, as shown, to create the top of your figure.

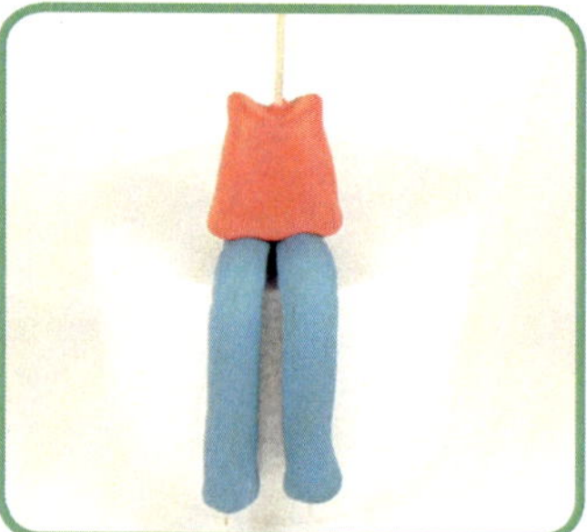

22 Push this onto your skewer, gluing all pieces.

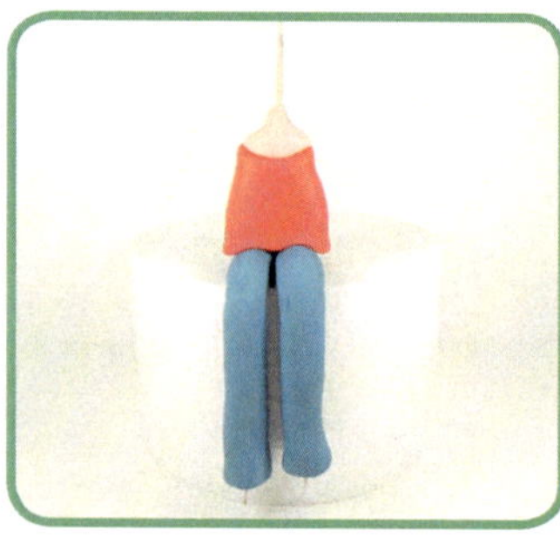

23 Create a flesh coloured chest/neck piece but allow to dry fully before attaching the head.

24 Roll a thin length of contrasting paste to trim your figure's t-shirt...

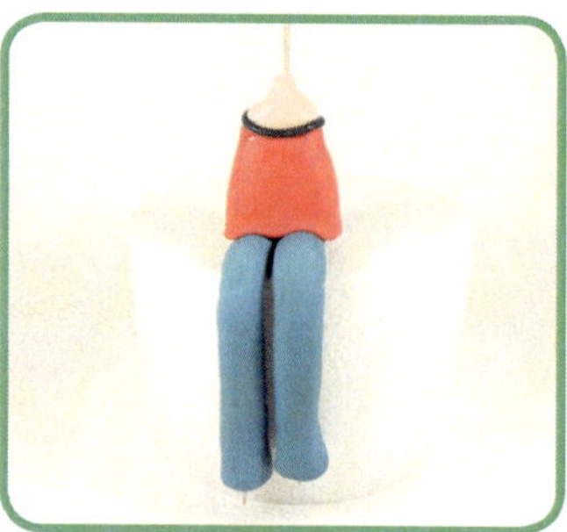

25 ...attach, as shown.

26 Roll a ball of flesh coloured paste to form a head.

27 Push slightly with your thumb to form the face shape.

28 Add a mouth (scallop tool) and nose (small ball of flesh coloured paste). Attach the head and body only when both are suitably dry.

29 Create two small ears by rolling two tiny balls of paste and indenting with a small ball tool.

30 Create eye sockets by pressing gently with a small ball tool. Roll two small balls of black paste and glue in place.

31 Add tiny white non-pareils.

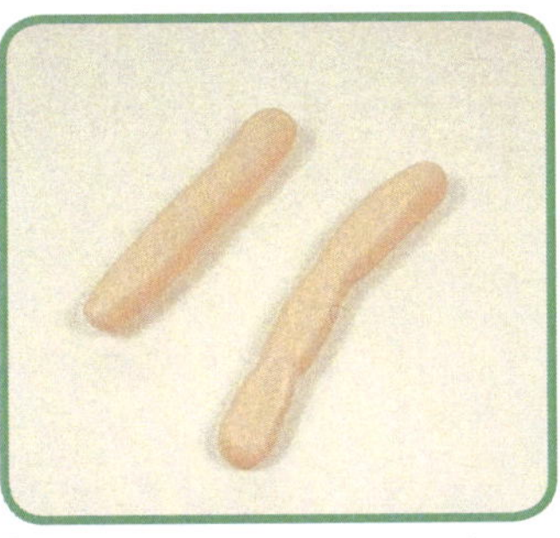

32 Roll two flesh coloured sausage shapes to form the arms. Pinch to form an elbow, wrist and hand, as shown.

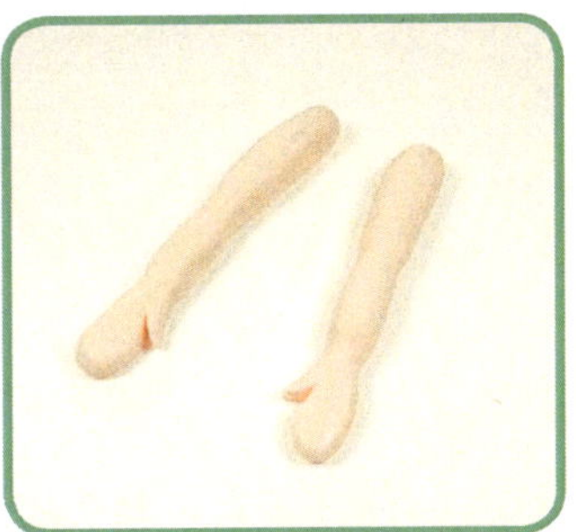

33 Use a scalpel tool to create thumbs...

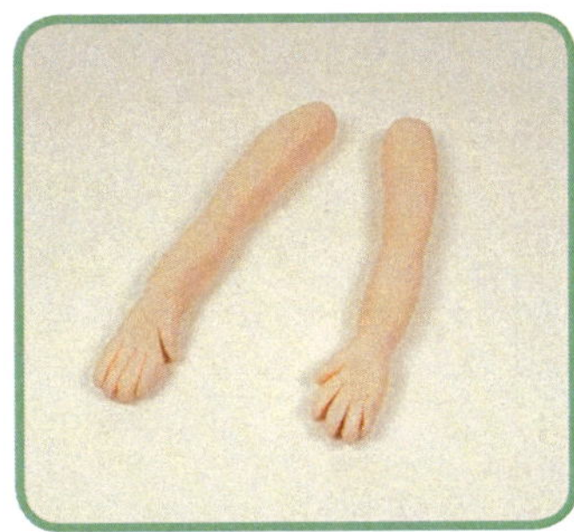

34 ...and three further cuts will create fingers

35 Attach the arms to the body.

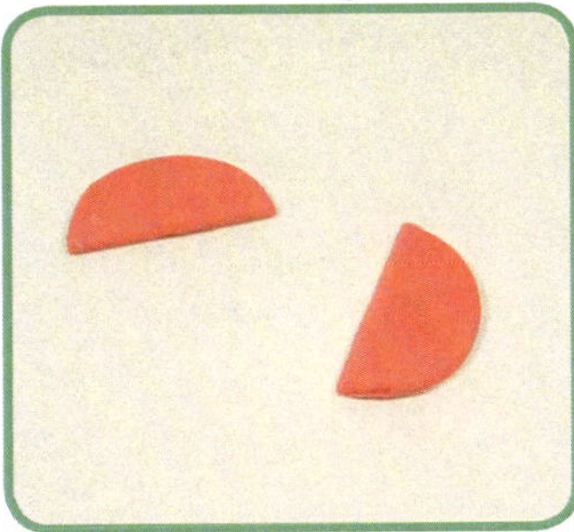

36 If you'd like to add sleeves, cut a small circle of paste then cut in half. Place over the tops of the arms (see Step 38).

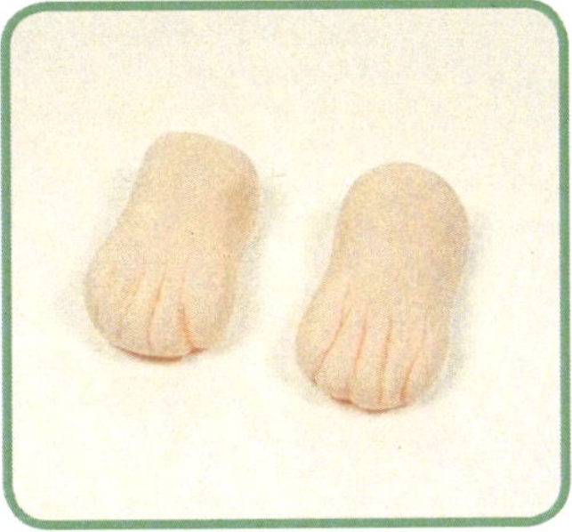

37 Create simple feet using a pad of paste with toes marked using a veining tool.

38 Attach these to the tooth-picks and glue in place. You may want to support these while they dry in place.

39 Create the hair by cutting a rectangular piece of paste. Add texture with a veining tool in a random vertical pattern.

40 Fix this to the rear of the head - don't worry if it looks a little odd at this stage!

41 Cut an approximate semi-circle of paste and mark a fringe (bangs) with your veining tool.

42 Attach around the head.

43 Cut a slim band of coloured paste and add to create a hairband.

44 Make a simple bow by cutting a small rectangle of paste, pinching in the middle then wrapping a further piece of paste around the centre.

45 Attach to the hairband for instant prettiness!

46 Add little details like eye-lashes (black edible paint applied with a fine detail brush) and rosy cheeks (a dusting of pink petal dust).

Teen Queen Cupcakes

Materials

Cupcake topper discs
Modelling paste:
Black, White,
Green, Yellow,
Red, Grey,
Red, Blue,
Brown, Black
Edible paint: silver, white
Edible pen: black
Edible glue

Tools

Craft knife/scalpel
Veining tool
Veining tool
Ball tool
Large flat knife
Cocktail straw
Small blossom cutter
Fine paintbrush

1 For the hair straighteners, roll a slim sausage of black paste (to fit on your cupcake topper disc) and trim slightly at one end.

2 Cut a slit down the centre.

3 Cut two small rectangles of sand coloured paste to fit, as shown.

4 Roll two small balls of black paste. Press one onto the rear of the straighteners and one at the end of the slit, as pictured.

5 Finally, roll a long thin length of black paste to form the flex.

6 Attach all to the cupcake disc and add painted silver detail.

7 For the hairdryer, roll two long teardrop shapes of paste, as pictured. Cut the smaller piece diagonally across the top.

8 Use your veining tool to create the filter detail at the rear of the hairdryer.

9 Use your knife to trim the front of the hairdryer.

10 To create a nozzle, cut a flat-topped triangle, as shown. Use your fingers to press this into a wedge shape at the front.

11 Roll a thin length of black paste to form the flex.

12 Attach all to the cupcake disc and add painted silver detail.

13 To create the laptop, cut a rectangle of grey paste, creating a seam across the centre.

14 Cut three rectangular shapes, as shown, from black paste. Do not attach yet.

15 Use your flat knife to lightly press a keyboard pattern into the appropriate piece of paste, taking care not to cut right through.

16 Fold the grey piece of paste and rest against a flat surface to dry. Paint with bright silver edible paint.

17 Now attach the black pieces, adding tiny details with white edible paint.

18 To create the i-pad, cut a thin rectangle of black paste.

19 To create the i-pad, cut a thin rectangle of black paste.

20 Lay this over the top of piece of white paste and trim, leaving a slim frame of white paste all around and deeper at the bottom.

21 Use a cocktail straw to gently imprint a function bottom at the bottom.

22 Paint details using white edible paint and a black edible ink pen.

23 To create a book, cut a deep rectangle of white paste.

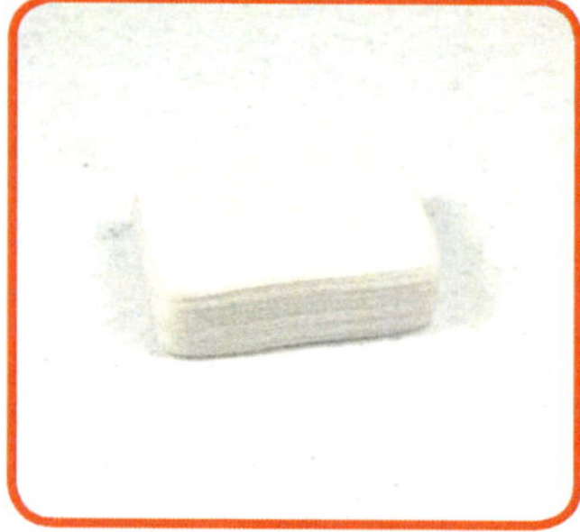

24 Use the edge of your knife to imprint 'pages' on three sides.

25 Lay the page piece on a long rectangle of coloured paste and trim, as shown.

26 Flip over...

27 ...and trim. Using your veining tool/knife, gently create spine details on your book.

28 You can write a title directly onto your book or add a small white plaque of white paste.

29 To create the cola can, roll a small cylinder of red paste.

30 Use a veining tool to create the neck of the can.

31 Add detail with edible silver and white paints.

32 Create a chocolate bar by cutting a small rectangle of brown paste and imprinting the squares with your knife.

33 Create a 'bite mark' with your blossom cutter!

34 For the crisps/potato chips packet, roll a thin rectangle of coloured paste.

35 Fold over, attaching the sides at the back and pressing the base with your fingers.

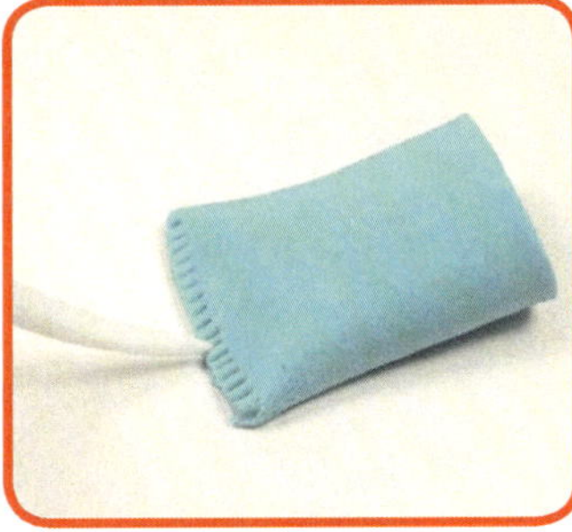

36 Use your veining tool to create a 'seal' at the bottom. Open the 'packet' wide at the top.

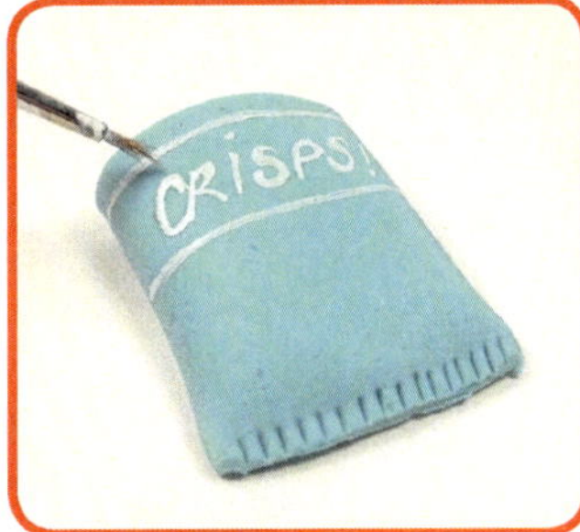

37 Add painted details as you like!

38 Make little crisps/potato chips by rolling tiny balls of sand coloured paste. Shape these using a ball tool.

39 To make headphones, cut a flat strip of black paste for the headband. Form a curve, as shown.

40 Make two small pads to form the 'over-ear' pieces.

41 Use your veining tool to create creases and your ball tool to add detail too.

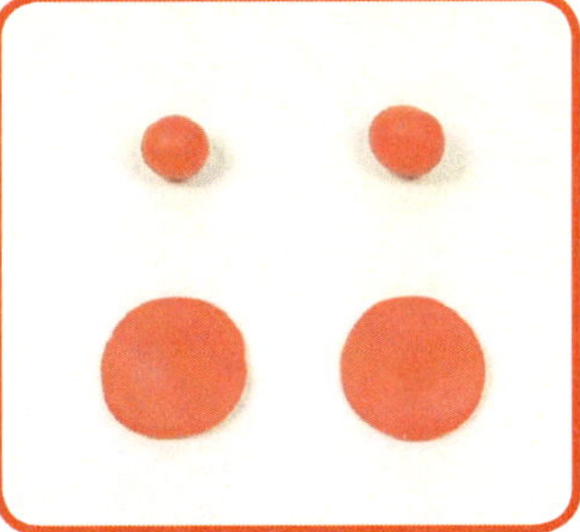

42 You can add colour to the headphones by rolling two small balls of paste then flattening to form headphone covers.

43 Attach all to your topper disc, as shown.

44 Roll a thin length of black paste – trim to fit.

45 Add tiny painted details as you like!

46 Gadget designs can be very black and masculine so to 'pretty them up', add tiny coloured blossoms and use colourful topper discs too!

Mini Make-Up Cupcakes

Materials

Modelling paste: Baby pink, Black, White, Grey, Tan, Green, Purple, Red
Blush x 3
Cupcake topper discs
Edible paint: silver, white
Petal dusts: various
Confectioners glaze
Edible glue

Tools

Craft knife/scalpel
Round cutters
Veining tool
Paintbrushes
Black cocktail straw
Scriber tool

1 To create the single eye shadow, form a pad of black paste, approx. 5mm thick.

2 Cut a circle of approx. 40mm/1½" wide from this.

3 Cut and remove a smaller circle, approx. 30mm/1¼", leaving you with a round outer frame

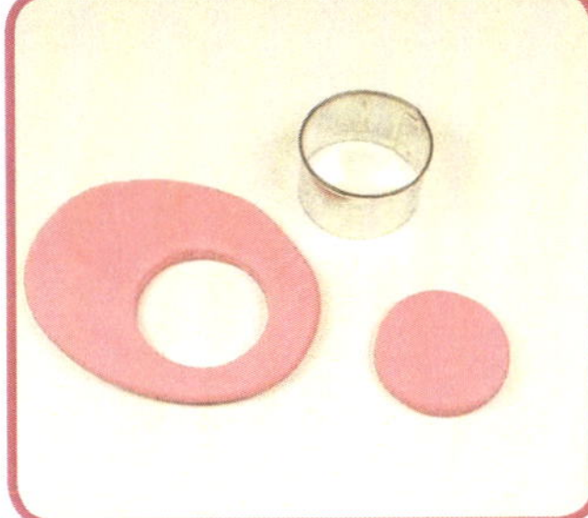

4 In the colour of your choice, cut a circle in the same size as Step 3.

5 Insert this into the round frame.

6 To create the applicator, roll a small sausage shape of black paste and a small oval of white paste.

7 Dust the tip of the 'applicator' with petal dust in the same colour as the eyeshadow and attach both to your cupcake topper disc.

8 To create the blusher brush, roll a sausage shape of black paste and trim at each end.

9 Use your veining tool to create two notches across one end of this piece.

10 Use cream coloured paste to create the brush head, forming this into a large sweetcorn niblet shape!

11 Use your scriber tool to create the effect of bristles.

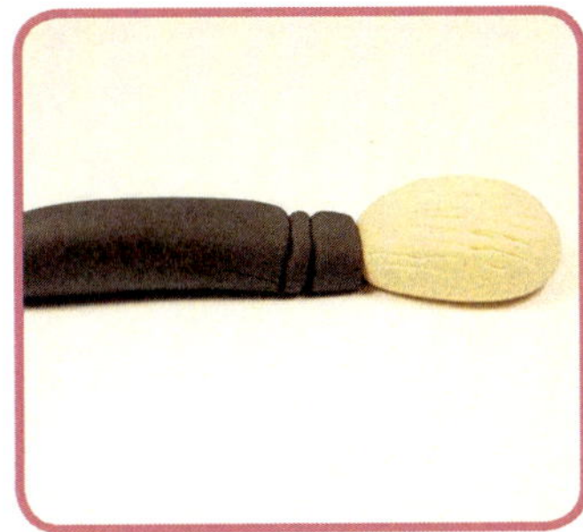

12 Lay both pieces together to ensure they fit, pressing down on the neck of the brush to ensure they meet in height.

13 Paint the neck of your brush with edible silver paint.

14 Dust the tip of your blusher brush with peach/pink edible petal dust.

15 To create false eyelashes, cut two slim flat rectangles of black paste.

16 Use your scalpel tool to cut 'lashes'. Keep your tool flat and pull towards you to prevent breakage.

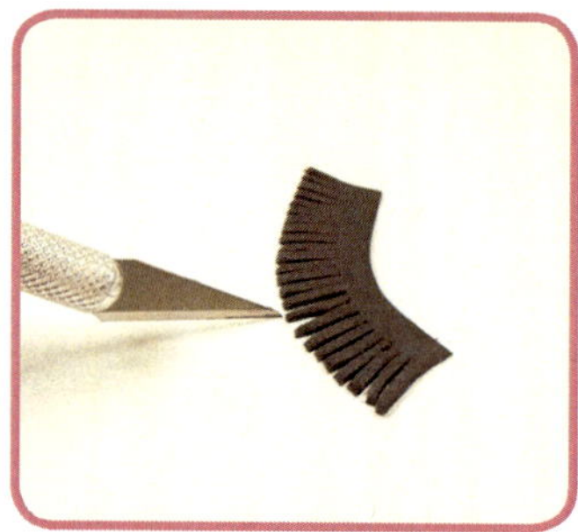
17 Use the tip of your scalpel tool to lightly separate the lashes.

18 Carefully form the lashes over the edge of an upturned cup and leave to dry.

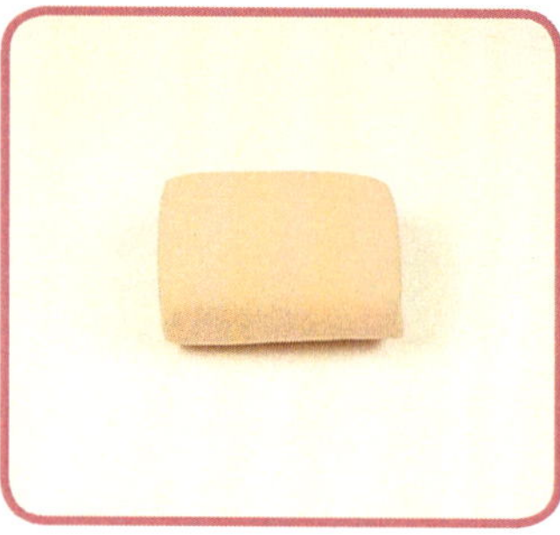
19 To create the foundation tube, roll a fat sausage of paste, trimming at either end.

20 Gently flatten at one end and use your fingers to lightly fan it out slightly.

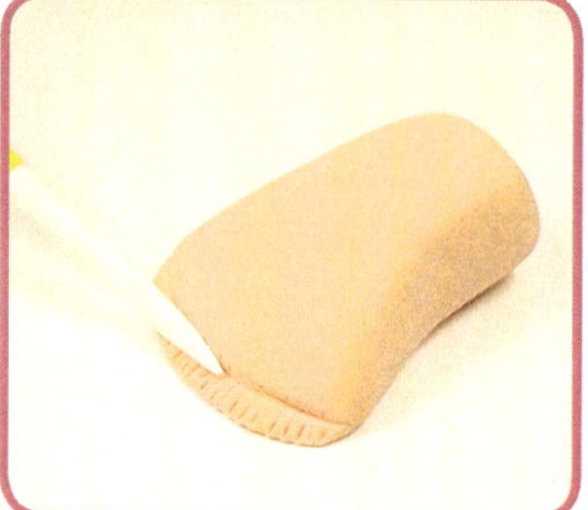
21 Use your veining tool to create a seam at the flattened end...

22 ...and use in an upwards direction to create notches along the top.

23 Roll a sausage of black paste, trim at one end then cut a 'slice' from the sausage.

24 Attach this to the base of your foundation tube to create a 'lid'.

25 To create the lipstick, roll a sausage of black paste, trimming at one end. Cut a piece from this end to form the base.

26 Roll the remaining sausage to make it a little narrower and cut two pieces, as shown.

27 Glue all pieces together, as shown, and allow to dry. Paint the narrower pieces with edible silver paint.

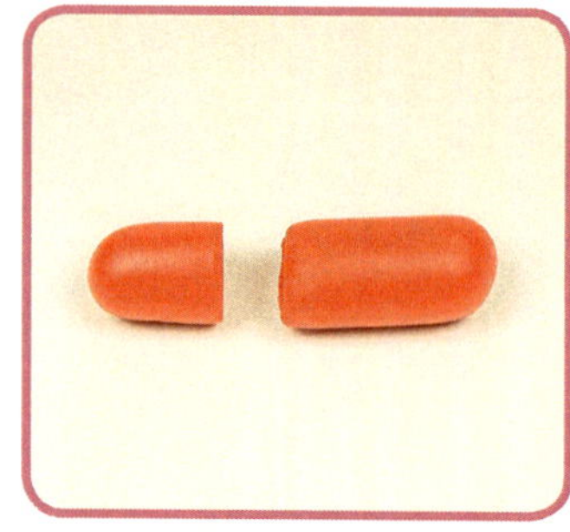
28 Roll a sausage of paste in the lipstick colour of your choice! Cut to size.

29 Shape this into a lipstick 'bullet' shape and attach to your topper disc.

30 To create the powder compact, cut two squares of paste approx. 40mm/1½".

31 Cut a circle of approx. 30mm/1¼" from the centre of one square.

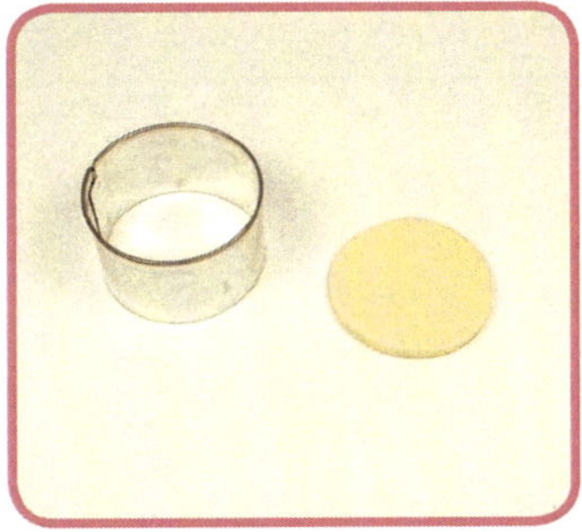

32 Cut a 30mm/1¼" circle of cream coloured paste to create the powder insert...

33 ...and a further 30mm/1¼" circle of white paste to create your powder puff.

34 Attach all items to your topper disk, as shown. Make sure that your 'lid' piece has dried firmly. Dust the 'puff' with cream petal dust.

35 To create the multi-eye shadow palette, cut a square of black paste. Cut this in half.

36 Cut three rectangles of contrasting paste to fit within one half...

37 ...and a rectangle of light grey paste to fit the other.

38 Paint irregular diagonal lines across the grey paste to create a 'mirror' effect.

39 Attach items, as shown, ensuring that your 'lid' piece has dried firmly.

40 To create the mascara, roll a small sausage of black paste. Trim at both ends.

41 Use sharp scissors to cut little spikes. Work from bottom to top in vertical rows.

42 Roll a sausage shape of coloured paste and trim at each end to create the wand handle.

43 Insert the cocktail straw into the mascara end and attach. Insert into the handle end and trim to size before attaching.

44 You can create a mascara 'swoosh' on your topper using a flat brush and some black food colour!

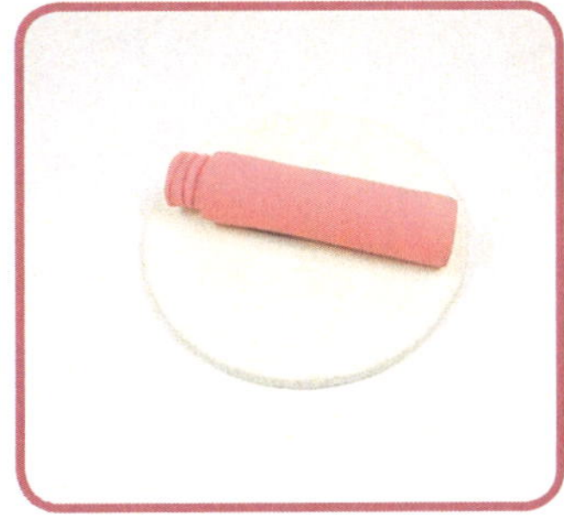

45 Or simply add a mascara 'tube' by creating one in the same way as the wand handle.

46 Use your detail brush and some edible black/white paint to add detail to your items. Confectioner's glaze can also add shine.

Tiffany Cake Collection

Materials

Rice Krispie treats
Modelling paste:
White
Aqua
Lustre dust: pearl
Edible paint: silver
Piping gel
Edible glue

Tools

Craft knife/scalpel
Ruler
Scriber tool
Large flat knife
Quilting tool
Veining tool
Tiny letter stamps
Heart shaped cutter
Small round cutters
Round cutters: 68mm & 78mm (2¾" & 3")
Foam cupcake domes (optional)

1 Create a cube of Rice Krispie treats in the size you wish for your gift box – ensure it fits on top of your cake!

2 Cut four squares of paste (plus another for the lid) slightly larger than the sides of your cube. Leave to dry.

3 Hold the first piece against your cube and trim to size across the top only (mark with scriber tool and cut with scalpel tool and ruler).

4 Hold the next piece against the first, as shown, and again trim to size.

5 Repeat with the third side, as shown.

6 Make two small marks, as shown, on each of your side pieces. This will allow for your fourth side to be added.

7 Now that your first three sides are trimmed to fit, brush one side of each panel with edible glue and attach.

8 Holding the fourth side, mark your final cuts with a scriber tool. Trim using ruler and scalpel tool.

9 Now place your shape on top of the fifth panel, the base, and trim using a large, flat knife.

10 Cut four rectangles of paste, longer than the sides of your box. These will form the edges of your 'lid'.

11 To cut the correct size, butt each rectangle up against the next around each side of the box, and trimming accordingly.

12 For the top of the lid roll more of the same Tiffany blue paste. Leave to dry.

13 Place your upside down box on top and trim using a large, flat knife. This will be the lid piece.

14 Glue the top and edges of the lid in place, supporting while the sides set.

15 For the ribbon, cut four long, flat strips of white paste. Add stitch detail to the sides with the quilting tool. Glue up, across and down the middle of the box, as shown.

16 Do the same on the opposite side to create a crossed ribbon effect.

17 The 'ribbon' is now in place, and needs a nice bow!

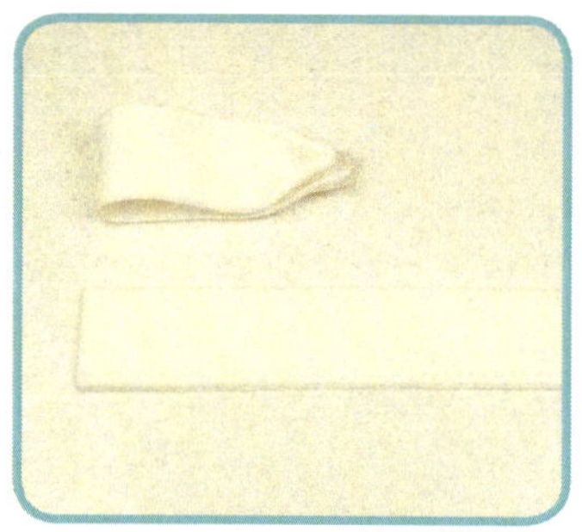

18 To create a bow, cut two further strips of paste (same size as your 'ribbon', above). Fold each strip over and pinch.

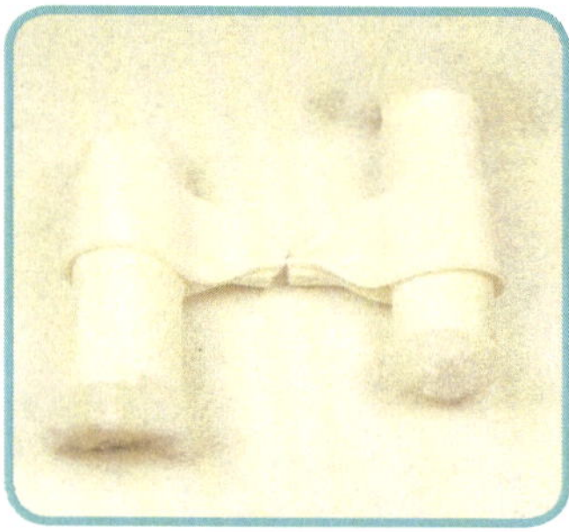

19 While they dry, it helps to fill them with kitchen paper so that they hold their shape.

20 When dry, cut a smaller flat strip of paste and wrap around the join of your bow. Attach all pieces together.

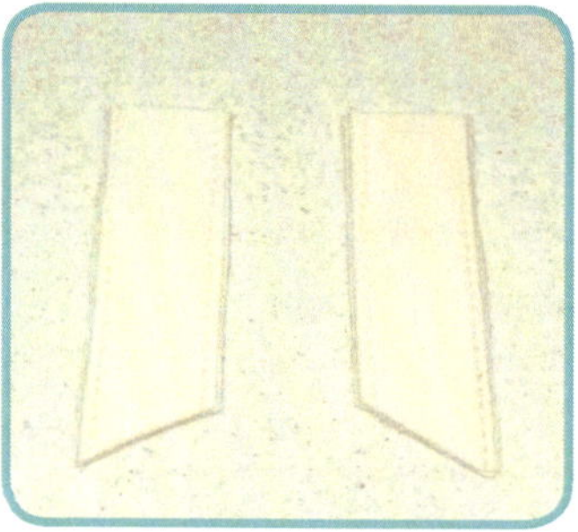

21 Finally, for the tails of your bow, cut two further flat strips of paste. Trim both at opposing angles at one end. Add stitched detail to edges.

22 For the Tiffany locket, roll a piece of white paste. Use tiny letter stamps to create a brand/recipient's name etc. Stamp the paste.

23 Cut a heart shape from your stamped paste.

24 Cut two thin strips of paste, as shown.

25 Create a u-shape with one piece and attach to the back of your heart shape. Trim as required.

26 Hook the second strip through the first, pressing the ends together lightly.

27 Finally, paint your pendant with bright silver edible paint.

28 Assemble all pieces together. Use your veining tool to gently insert your heart pendant under the bow.

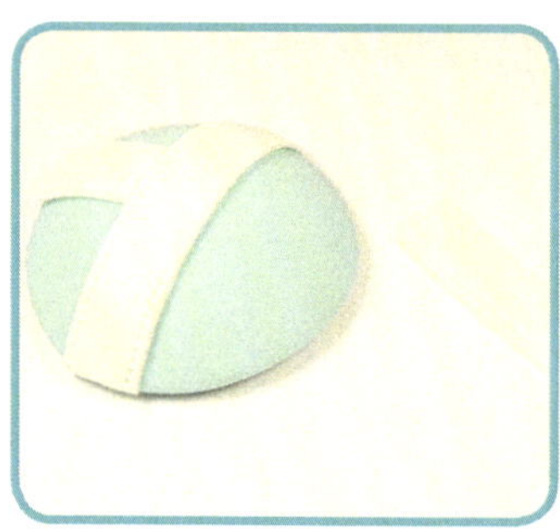

29 For a pretty bow cupcake, start with a 78mm (3") round paste disc dried over a formed cupcake dome. Use strips of paste to form a cross shape.

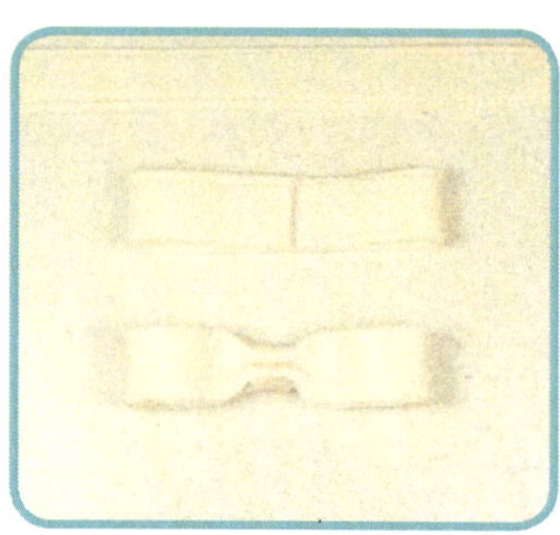

30 To form a simple bow, cut a strip of white paste. Fold this over into the middle and pinch in the centre. Follow Steps 20 and 21 to complete.

31 Assemble all on your cupcake dome, supporting the loops of your bow while they dry into shape.

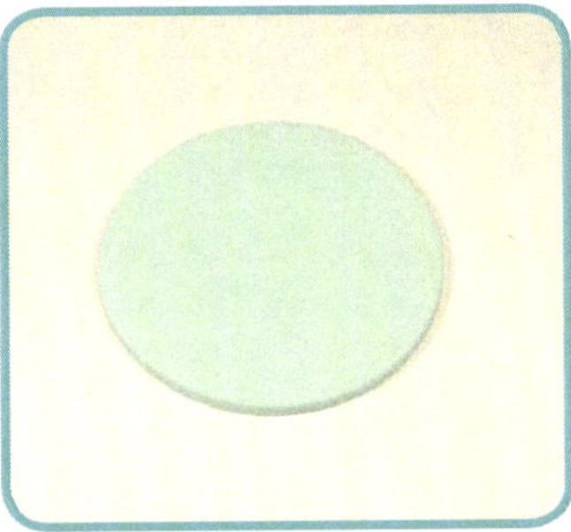

32 For the multi-looped bow topper, start with a 68mm (2 ¾”) flat round disc, which has been dried.

33 Cut 11 x flat strips of white paste.

34 Add stitching detail to each strip.

35 Loop each piece over, pinching at the end, as shown.

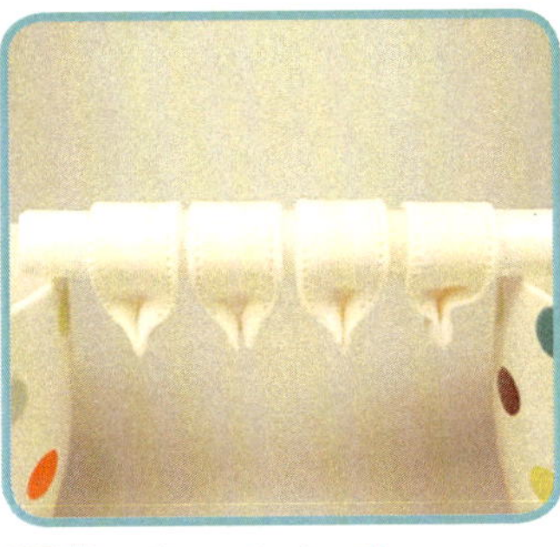

36 Top tip – drying these over a tube shape (we've used a thick poly dowel) really helps!

37 Attach the first six pieces to your cupcake disk.

38 Add four further pieces, as shown. Glue in place as you go.

39 Glue your final loop to the centre to complete the design.

40 To create the pearl pendant design, create the heart using Steps 22-27, as above. This time however create TWO links through your pendant (shown).

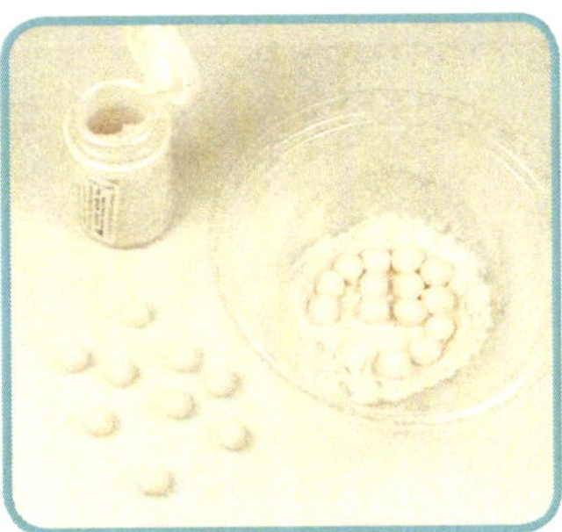

41 Roll small equal size balls of paste and roll these in pearl lustre dust.

42 Attach the pendant to your disk, trimming the ‘tails’ of silver loops. Start to add the pearls.

43 Repeat on the other side to complete, gluing each pearl in place.

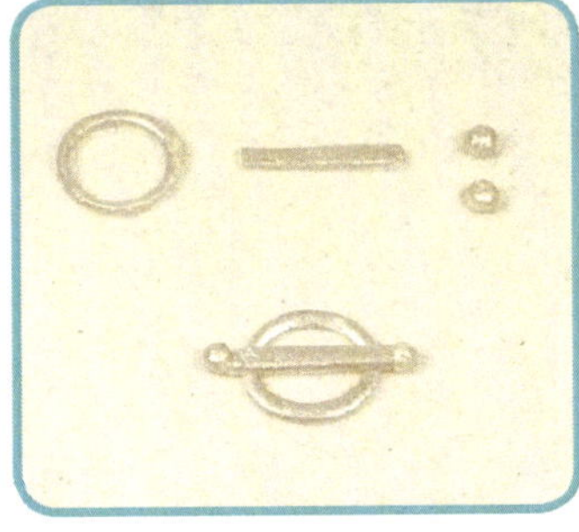

44 To create the bracelet, cut a small round empty circle, a small flat strip, and roll two tiny balls. Paint all silver. Create a ‘fastening’, as shown.

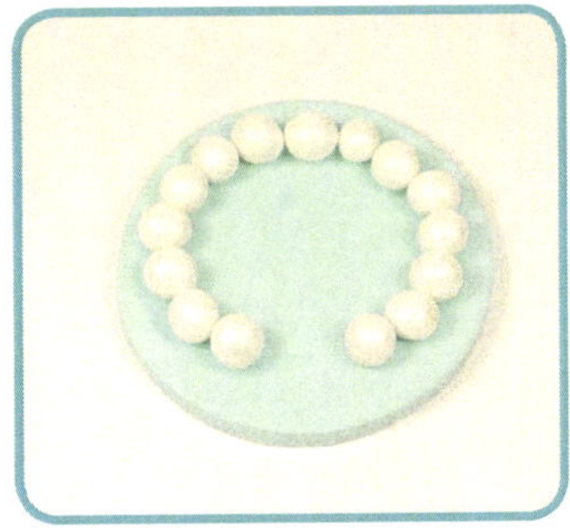

45 Form an open circle of pearls (Step 41) on a 68mm (2 ¾”) flat cupcake topper disk.

46 Finally, attach your bracelet fastening.

Fashion Sewing Cupcakes

Materials

Modelling paste:
Light brown, Cream,
Baby pink, Baby blue,
Yellow, Red
White
Cupcake topper discs
Edible pen: black
Edible paint: silver
Edible glue

Tools

Craft knife/scalpel
Round cutters, various
Cone tool
Lollipop stick

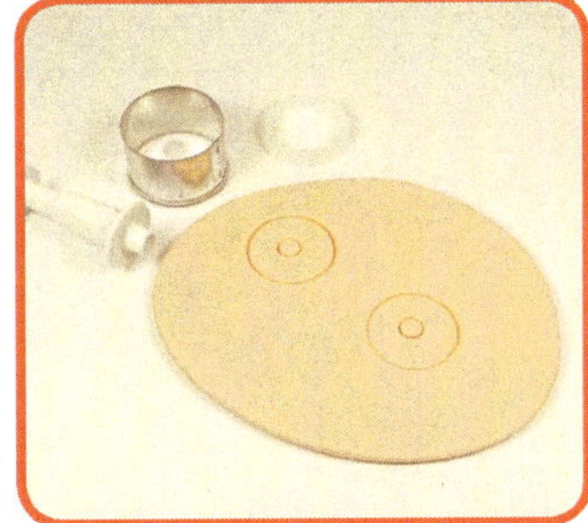

1 Roll a piece of dark beige paste. Make circular indentations using the round cutters, as shown.

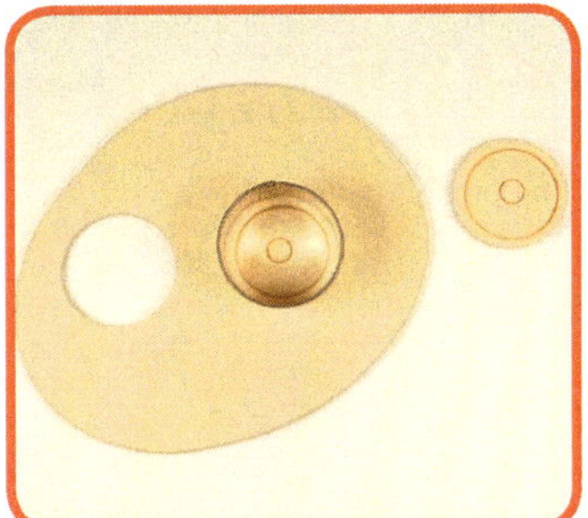

2 Place a third larger cutter over the top of these indentations and cut out

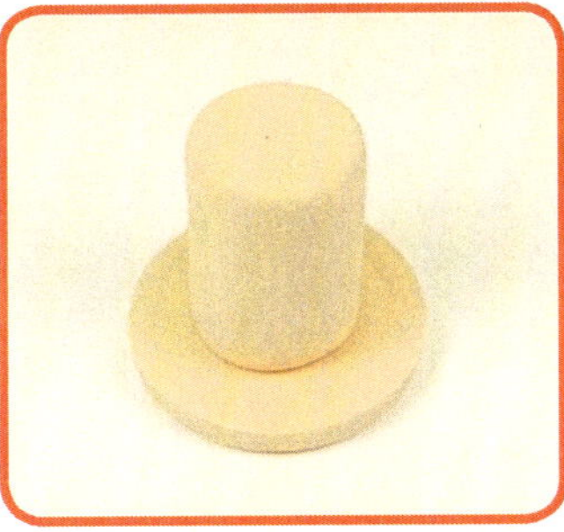

3 Roll a sausage of the same colour paste and trim flat at either end. Attach to one of circle cuts, as shown.

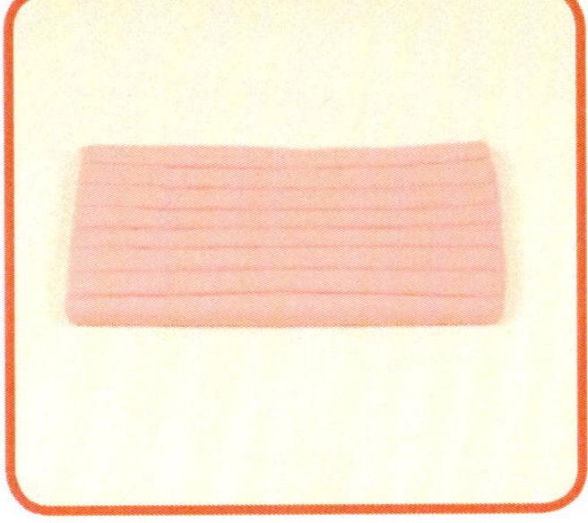

4 Create a piece of rectangular paste the same height as the 'post' of your bobbin and long enough to wrap around it. Mark lines to suggest threads.

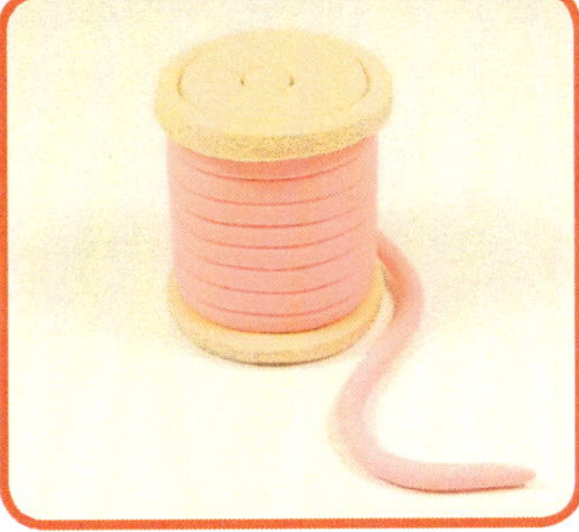

5 Wrap and glue this to the bobbin. Attach the second circle to the top. Roll and glue on a thin sausage of paste, coiling around to suggest thread

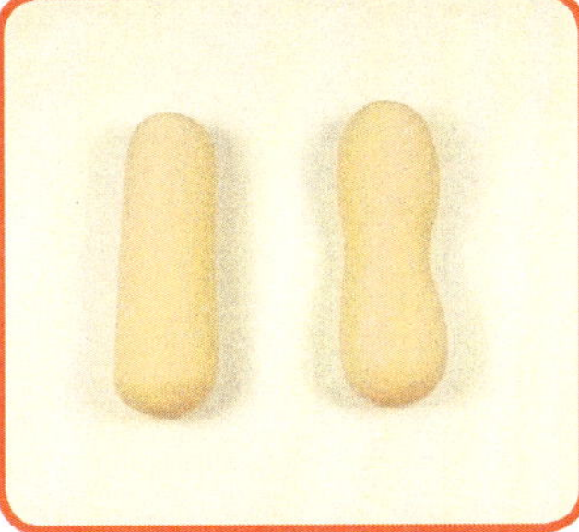

6 For the dressmaker's form, roll a sausage of dark beige paste. Squeeze lightly in the centre (the waist), as shown.

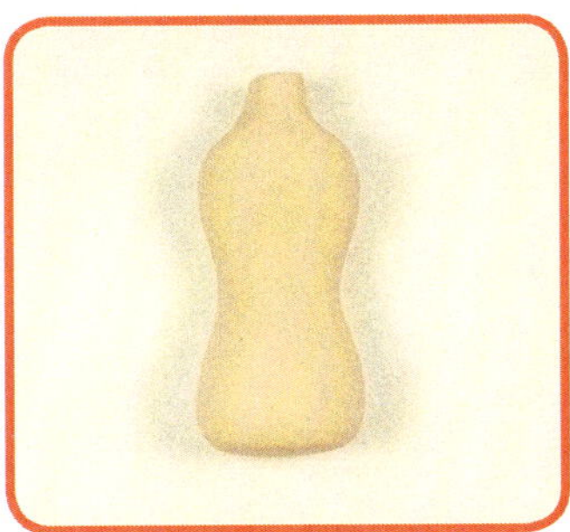

7 Use your fingers to form into the shape shown.

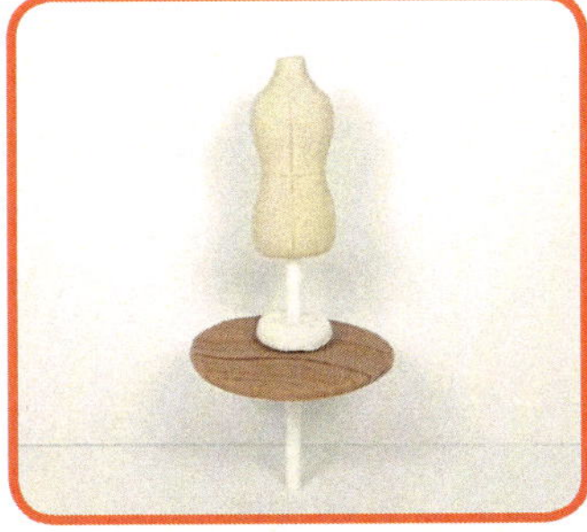

8 Insert lolly stick and cut to size – you may want this to extend into your cupcake to provide stability. Cut a small circle for the base and mark with veining tool.

9 Use a ribbon cutter or ruler to create a length of paste to make your measuring tape.

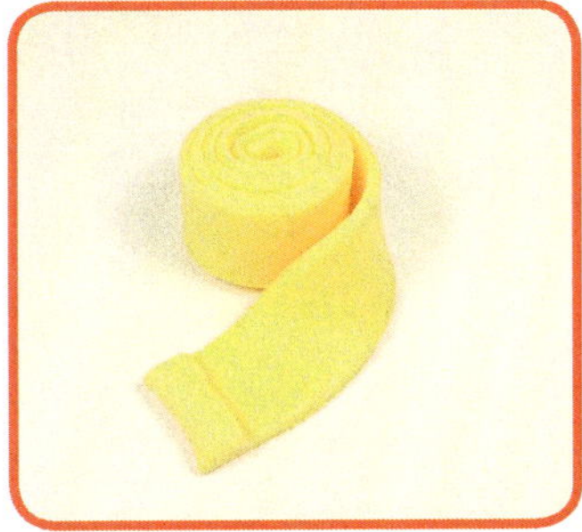

10 Coil this around, leaving one end loose. Turn one end back on itself and allow to dry.

11 Use your edible pen to mark measurements. Paint the folded edge of your 'tape' silver.

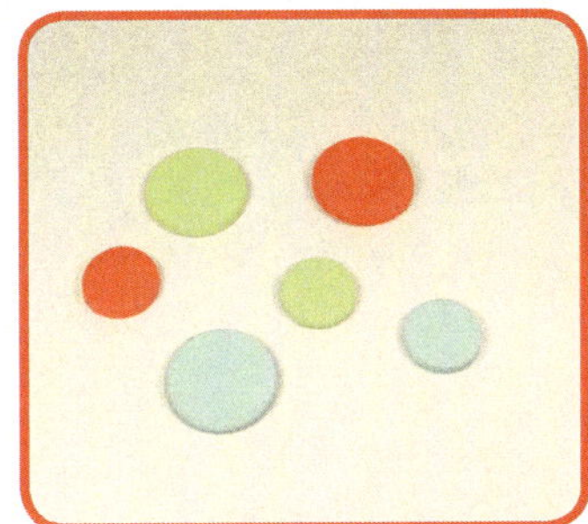

12 Cut a selection of round pieces to create buttons.

13 Use a smaller circle cutter on each piece to create an inner indentation. Use a cone tool to create 'holes' in your buttons.

14 Use buttons on their own or to accessorise other toppers.

Summer Fashion Cupcakes

Materials

Modelling paste:
Red
Blue
Sand/ Yellow
White
Black
Edible paint: white
Edible glue

Tools

Craft knife/scalpel
Round cutter: 68mm (2 ¾")
Toothpicks
Quilting tool
Veining tool
Small circle and oval cutter sets
Heart cutter set
Blossom cutter

1 For the cupcake discs, roll a piece of sand coloured paste and texturise all over with a bunch of toothpicks secured with an elastic band.

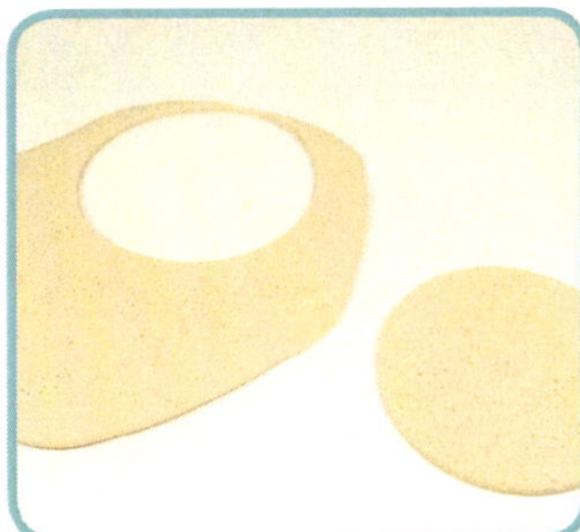

2 Cut each disc with a 68mm (2¾") round cutter and leave to dry firm.

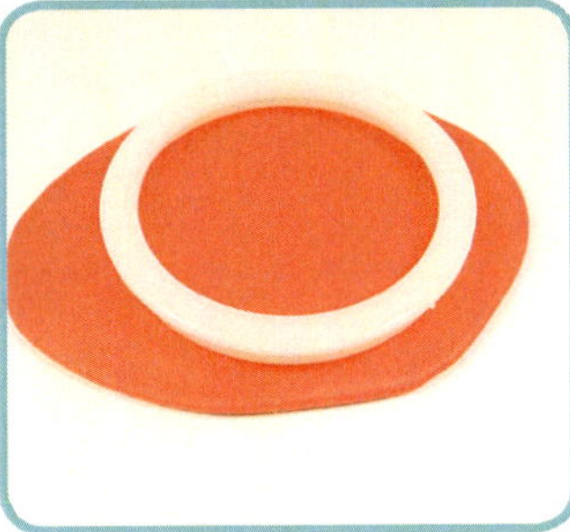

3 To make the bikini bottoms, cut a circle of red paste (which will fit within your cupcake topper).

4 Cut the waistband with a slightly round shape (we've used an oval cutter - top) and each leg with the edge of a round cutter.

5 Use your quilting tool to add detail to the leg and waist area.

6 For the bikini top, cut a piece of paste with a large blossom cutter, as shown, or...

7 ...use a heart shaped cutter instead.

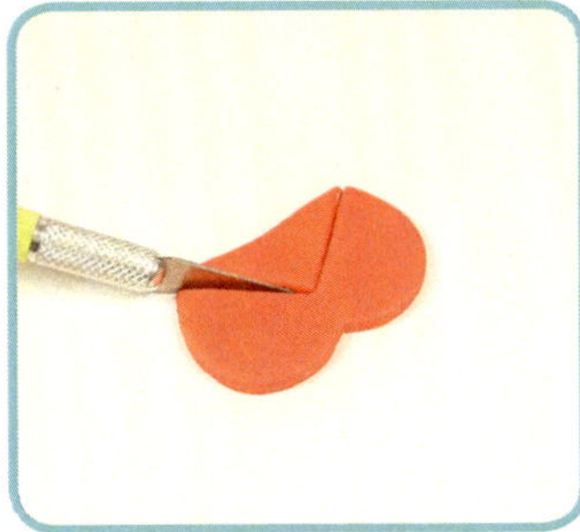

8 Use your scalpel tool to cut a bikini top shape, as shown.

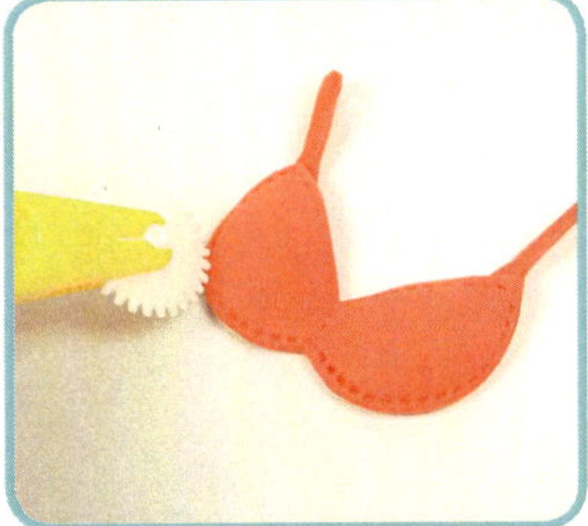

9 Cut two small strips of red paste to use as straps and add detail with your stitching tool.

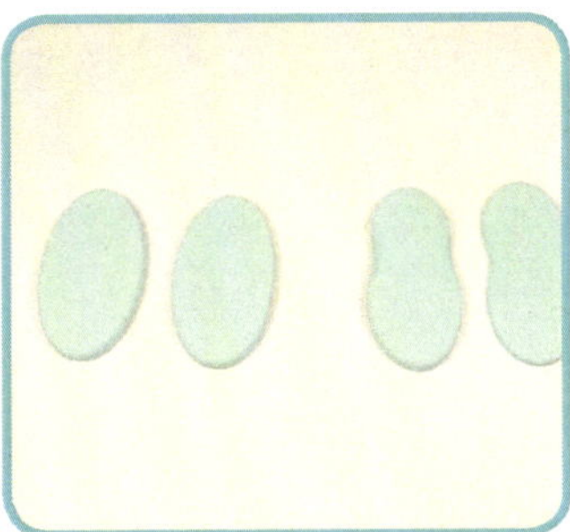

10 For the flip flops, cut two ovals of equal size and pinch lightly to create the shape shown.

11 Cut two thin strips of contrasting paste, pinch each one in the centre and carefully add to your flip flops, as shown.

12 For the sunglasses, cut a piece of paste using the top of a heart shaped cutter.

13 Use your fingers and a veining tool to form a sunglasses shape, as shown.

14 Cut a small oval shape of black paste in half. Shape lightly with your fingers to create each lens. Add detail with small flowers and white edible paint.

Large Shoe Templates

HEEL

SOLE

FRONT

Made in the USA
Middletown, DE
09 April 2015